IT'S IN THE ACTION

IT'S IN THE ACTION

Memories of a Nonviolent Warrior

C. T. VIVIAN

WITH STEVE FIFFER

FOREWORD BY ANDREW YOUNG

NewSouth Books

Montgomery

NewSouth Books
105 S. Court Street
Montgomery, AL 36104

Library of Congress Cataloging-in-Publication Data

Names: Vivian, C. T., author. | Fiffer, Steve, author. | Young, Andrew, 1932- writer of
foreword.

Title: It's in the action : memories of a nonviolent warrior / C.T. Vivian with Steve
Fiffer ; foreword by Andrew Young.

Other titles: It is in the action

Description: Montgomery, AL : NewSouth Books, [2021] | Includes bibliographical
references and index. | Summary: "C. T. Vivian's life was never defined by the
discrimination and hardship he faced, although there were many instances of both
throughout his lifetime. The late civil rights leader instead focused on his faith in God and
his steadfast belief in nonviolence, extending these principles nationwide as a member
of the Southern Christian Leadership Conference. It's in the Action contains Vivian's
recollections, ranging from finding religion at the young age of five to his imprisonment
as part of the Freedom Rides. The late civil rights leader's heart-wrenching and inspiring
stories from a lifetime of nonviolent activism come just in time for a new generation of
activists, similarly responding to systems of injustice, violence, and oppression. It's in the
Action is a record of a life dedicated to selflessness and morality, qualities achieved by
Vivian that we can all aspire to." — provided by publisher.

Identifiers: LCCN 202005142 (print) | LCCN 202005143 (ebook) | ISBN
9781588384416 (hardcover) | ISBN 9781588384423 (ebook)

Subjects: LCSH: Vivian, C. T. | African American civil rights workers—Biography. |
Civil rights workers—United States—Biography. | African American clergy—Biography. |
Civil rights movements—Southern States—History—20th century. | African Americans—
Civil rights. | Nonviolence—United States—History. | Southern States—Race relations.

Classification: LCC E185.97.V58 A3 2021 (print) | LCC E185.97.V58 (ebook) | DDC
323.092 [B]—dc23

LC record available at https://lccn.loc.gov/202005142LC
ebook record available at https://lccn.loc.gov/202005143

Printed in the United States of America by Sheridan

The Black Belt, defined by its dark, rich soil, stretches across central
Alabama. It was the heart of the cotton belt. It was and is a place of great
beauty, of extreme wealth and grinding poverty, of pain and joy. Here we
take our stand, listening to the past, looking to the future.

To my wife, who persevered and continued
to love and care throughout the years of my being away
from home for the sake of the struggle,
who continued to raise our children and transferred
to them even in the presence of radical evil
the faith that we both hold in God and man.

— C. T. V.

Do to us what you will and we will still love you.

— MARTIN LUTHER KING JR.

Contents

Foreword

ANDREW YOUNG

C. T. Vivian loved words—spoken or written. In fact, it's probably not an exaggeration to say that the only thing C. T. loved more than words was his family: his wife, Octavia, his children, his grandchildren, and yes, his great-grandchildren.

Before he received his true calling from a higher being, C. T. thought his calling was to be a journalist. He would have been a great one. Because he could turn a phrase like he could turn the other cheek. And he could quote our great poets—from Phillis Wheatley to Langston Hughes—and thinkers—from Du Bois to Ellison—as readily as he could quote Scripture.

His love of the written word is reflected in his collection of more than six thousand volumes—fiction, nonfiction, and poetry—written by African Americans about the Black experience. As his daughter Denise Morse told the *Atlanta Journal-Constitution*: "Growing up, we had books everywhere. On every table, stacked in the corners. He and Mom would get in a car and drive to California, stopping at little bookstores along the way. They would come home with a trunkload of books."

I'm happy to report that the C. T. and Octavia Vivian Library will be housed within the base of the 110-foot Peace Column in the upcoming Rodney Cook Sr. Park in Atlanta's Vine City.

When C. T. took his own pen to paper he was as skillful as any of the writers in his vast collection. Witness his elegant, thoughtful portrait of Martin included at the end of this book. Consider, too, his first book, *Black Power and the American Myth*, equally thoughtful, but grittier.

In recent years it seems that anyone who passed through Washington, D.C., had a reality TV show, or "went viral" has written a memoir. Over the last half-century, C. T. certainly had the opportunity. I'm not sure why he waited so long. Maybe it was because he wasn't one to talk that much about himself, maybe he was too busy fighting the good fight, or maybe he wanted to wait until he had it all figured out.

I, for one, wish he'd started a little earlier than when he was in his nineties, but we're blessed to have *It's in the Action*—which while certainly chronicling C. T.'s actions in the movement also offers his thoughts on those actions. By this I mean that in the telling of his efforts in Peoria, Nashville, Chattanooga, Birmingham, St. Augustine, Selma, Chicago, and then Atlanta, he reflects upon the principles that guided him—love, faith, justice. Think of all those places! C. T.'s journey is a roadmap of the movement itself.

I feel honored to have called C. T. a friend and stood shoulder to shoulder with him. Now, thanks to *It's in the Action*, his words will live on forever, and new generations can stand on the shoulders of one of the great Americans of all time.

Andrew Young is a politician, diplomat, and pastor from Georgia who has served as mayor of Atlanta, congressman, and United States ambassador to the United Nations. He also served as president of the National Council of Churches USA and was a supporter and friend of Martin Luther King Jr. He lives in Atlanta.

Preface

STEVE FIFFER

C. T. Vivian was one of my heroes. It was, therefore, a thrill of a lifetime to interview him in 2014 about his days in Selma for a book I was writing with Adar Cohen: *Jimmie Lee & James: Two Lives, Two Deaths, and the Movement that Changed America.* He was a wonderful conversationalist and made me feel at ease immediately; he called me "Doc," as I later realized he called scores of others he interacted with.

Most surprising to me was that he said he envied my career. *My career!* Here was an icon of the civil rights movement, a man who had selflessly and bravely worked for changes that bettered the lives of so many Americans, a Presidential Medal of Freedom recipient, confessing that if he'd had his druthers he would have been a writer. Of course, if you listen to his sermons or speeches or his spontaneous remarks to the likes of Selma's infamous Sheriff Jim Clark or read his 1970 book, *Black Power and the American Myth*, you quickly realize he *was* a writer. But unlike the rest of us, he didn't always need pen or paper or typewriter or computer to make his words flow so eloquently. He could tell a story or tell off a racist antagonist with equal poetry.

After a few conversations, Dr. Vivian and I discussed the possibility of working together on his memoir. Nothing came of it. Then Atlanta announced that the C. T. and Octavia Vivian Library—featuring Dr. Vivian's extensive collection of African American literature dating back to colonial times—would be a centerpiece of its new Rodney Cook Sr. Park in Vine City. Dr. Vivian's daughter Denise Morse called and asked if we might revisit the idea of a memoir; the family thought it important, she said, that visitors to the C. T. and Octavia Vivian Library—as well as the rest of the world—know about the life of Dr. Vivian. I agreed.

By the time we started this effort, Dr. Vivian was approaching his ninety-fourth birthday. Understandably, his recall of events from his 1924 birth forward was not what it had once been. This circumstance complicated optimal participation in the writing of a first-person memoir—particularly when that person had been called "the greatest preacher ever to live" by Dr. Martin Luther King Jr. Fortunately, I had transcripts of my own interviews with him and of numerous other of his interviews and conversations with other parties—including the most gracious and generous Pulitzer Prize–winner Taylor Branch, PBS's *Eyes on the Prize* documentary series, and lengthy on-camera interviews with History Makers and the National Visionary Leadership Project. Videos of speeches and sermons also are bountiful, as are Dr. Vivian's own writings and numerous newspaper articles. (The papers of Dr. Vivian and his late wife Octavia—his rock and an author in her own right of a definitive biography of Coretta Scott King—can be found at Emory University in Atlanta.)

Thus, we were able to draw on Dr. Vivian's own words for this book. While some of those words were spoken several years earlier, this actually allowed for greater accuracy. Recollections—like those expressed to the makers of *Eyes on the Prize* about the Nashville Movement—twenty-five years after an event tend to be more accurate than memories shared with a writing partner fifty or sixty years after that event.

As the months went by, memories faded. The good news was that by that time we had covered the seminal years of the civil rights movement up through 1970. This included Dr. Vivian's pivotal role in integrating Peoria in 1947 and Nashville in 1960, where he worked with John Lewis, Diane Nash, and other movement stalwarts; his experience as a Freedom Rider beaten in Mississippi in 1961; his acceptance of MLK's invitation to take an executive role in the Southern Christian Leadership Conference and subsequent leadership of efforts in Birmingham (the Children's Crusade of 1963), St. Augustine (1964), and the push for a Voting Rights Act centered in Selma (1965); his creation of VISION, the forerunner of Upward Bound, that prepared hundreds of Black students (including Oprah Winfrey) for college; his journey to Chicago in 1966, when he foresaw that Northern cities would be the new civil rights battlegrounds and ministers needed to be trained for these battles; and his additional work in Chicago with gangs, labor unions, and the city itself to create thousands of jobs for people of color.

We had more we wanted to talk about: his return to the South, where in Atlanta he created innovative workshops to combat racism and foster workplace diversity; his creation of Seminary Without Walls; his travels around the world as a speaker and consultant; his prominent role in creating a Black bank in Atlanta; his reflections on the current state of affairs with regard to racism and economic disparity and his thoughts on how to address these and other inequities; his love of literature and collection of books; his thoughts on the most important figure in his professional life—Dr. King—and the philosophy of the movement; and, if this modest man could be coaxed to talk about it, his receipt of this nation's highest civilian award, the Presidential Medal of Freedom—presented by Barack Obama in 2013.

While we were unable to collaborate on chapters on these events, I have been able to put together three appendices that cover many of these achievements and reflections. Appendix 1, eulogies and remembrances at Dr. Vivian's funeral on July 23, 2020, by figures ranging from Joe Biden to Oprah Winfrey to Andrew Young to Hank Aaron to family members and business associates and his own pastor, also helps paint a more complete picture of the man and his activities in the years we were unable to cover in our interviews. Appendix 2 offers an overview of Dr. Vivian's activities and honors. Appendix 3, a 2015 interview on the fiftieth anniversary of Bloody Sunday, offers his reflections on the past, present, and future.

Many of the eulogists spoke about Dr. Vivian's humility—his commitment to achieving goals as opposed to achieving the spotlight. One story I came upon reflects that beautifully. In a 2014 article in the *Daily Beast*, former Obama staffer Joshua DuBois remembered an event in Selma in 2007.

The young senator was at Brown Chapel to worship and mark the anniversary of Bloody Sunday, the day in 1965 when civil rights activists faced dogs and batons as they marched from Selma to Montgomery. Obama took the pulpit to deliver a powerful sermon—one of my favorites, later called "The Joshua Generation" speech, in which he masterfully linked his own diverse lineage, the civil rights movement of the '50s and '60s, the journey of the people of Israel from Egypt to Canaan, and the political moment of that day.

But it was what happened before his formal remarks that really stood out to me. We staff had prepared a standard "acknowledgments card" for Obama to read, with the names of clergy, elected officials, and other dignitaries to thank before his speech. He read those acknowledgments, but when he was finished, Senator Obama said there was one more person who hadn't been recognized.

He looked out into the packed congregation and saw a wizened face sitting several pews back, an old man who looked to be well north of eighty years. None of the other speakers had noticed the man at that point, and we had not introduced him to Senator Obama before the service began. But Obama pointed to him and said, "And finally friends, here with us today is Dr. C. T. Vivian. Let's pause and thank him. That's the man Dr. Martin Luther King called the greatest preacher to ever live."

Vivian's smile grew wide and eyes teary at the unexpected acknowledgment. Several of us marveled at how we had missed the great Dr. Vivian—whose activism precipitated the 1965 march in the first place—and how Obama had picked his face out from so many others in the crowd.

Readers will observe that in a few instances, we resorted to contemporaneous newspaper accounts of events or reports by others in newspapers or books. We did so as infrequently as possible—only when we thought the account was more credible and accurate than Dr. Vivian's current memory. We have been sure to credit all such sources.

While we all may wish this memoir had been written years ago, we trust the pages that follow present a picture of the character and deeds of one of the true heroes of American history. In the years to come, we hope biographers and historians will complete that picture.

Acknowledgments

Because Dr. Vivian passed away before this book reached its final stage, it is left to me to acknowledge the many people who made this book possible. The Vivian Family deserves top billing. In particular, C. T. and Octavia's oldest child, Denise Morse, was the force driving the project forward and the source of counsel, content, and contacts. Jo Anna Vivian Walker and Carlton Morse were also important sources of information. Others on the Vivian team played major roles in the challenging task of making a posthumous memoir a reality. These included C. T.'s best friend and business partner Don Rivers; keeper of the Vivian photo archive Donald Bermudez; and Bill Smith of Jones Day in Atlanta. The role of the indefatigable Amanda Brown Olmstead cannot be overstated. She was assisted in her efforts by Mary Elise O'Brien.

John Hallwas, author, historian, friend of Dr. Vivian, and Distinguished Professor Emeritus at Western Illinois University, was a valuable source of support and information.

My literary agent Gail Hochman was influential in shaping my ideas about the book's structure, and my wife, Sharon Fiffer, was, as always, a valuable sounding board and reader. Adar Cohen, my co-author on another book about the civil rights era, provided excellent advice and helped with the early research, as did Ben Levine. Francesca Miroballi's timely transcription of my taped interviews and those of others kept us on schedule.

Every author should have the good fortune to work with a publishing house like NewSouth Books. The stewardship and vision of publisher Suzanne La Rosa and the knowledge and editorial expertise of Randall Williams (who knew Dr. Vivian years before I did!!!) made this a personal and professional dream experience. Matthew Byrne also played an important role. Thanks also to NewSouth staffers Lisa Emerson, Lisa Harrison, Beth Marino, Kelly Snyder, and Samantha Stanley.

As the Preface notes, due to circumstances beyond our control, we relied on past interviews for parts of the content. Special thanks to the generous Taylor Branch and the Smithsonian Institution, to Jim Hobart and the Legacy Project, to the History Makers, National Visionary Leadership Project, and the makers of perhaps the greatest documentary on the movement, *Eyes on the Prize*. The talented *Atlanta Journal-Constitution* reporter Ernie Suggs was also an invaluable and quotable source. Thanks also to those at First Kingdom Management for their constructive suggestions.

Advance praise from luminaries including Marian Wright Edelman, Bernard Lafayette, Jon Meacham, and Morris Dees was of great help in generating early interest in the book. And the Remembrances by Barack Obama, Joe Biden, Oprah Winfrey, Bernard Lafayette, Hank Aaron, Billye Aaron, Henrietta Antonin, and Andrew Young added great insight into Dr. Vivian. Extra thanks to Ambassador Young for his wonderful Foreword. The Reverend Gerald Durley—Dr. Vivian's good friend and pastor—also provided thoughtful insights in his stirring eulogy.

My final thanks go to Dr. Vivian himself, for being willing to share his important story with the world—a world made so much better by his commitment to three words: justice, truth, and love.

— S. F.

IT'S IN THE ACTION

On his hand, the ring with the crest Dr. Vivian designed.

Prologue

When We Came Out of Slavery

Friends, if you want to begin to understand me, my family, my people, I invite you to look at the ring with a family crest I designed years ago.

Do you see the blackness on the upper left with a handful of stars peeking through? That's slavery. We farmed the land in those dark days, but we did it under peonage, for others.

When we came out of slavery, we continued to farm. Because that was the work we knew. But it was different now that we were free. We didn't have to work for anyone else; and, when possible, we could buy farms for ourselves.

We were doing that, and we were winning, but then came the Great Depression. It knocked us down, but it didn't knock us out. Because during this time we were switching over to books, to knowledge. That's why my grandmother and my parents were so committed to the fact that no matter what happened, I was going to get an education. This is a commitment I've continued with my children and that they've continued with theirs.

You'll see that above the book that signifies learning, I've placed clouds. That's imagination. We don't learn solely by reading books. It's the imagination that goes with the education that creates something greater—the vision.

See the sun on the ring? It rises on a new day. And if you look closely, you'll see that it creates a cross.

The cross. That's what undergirded us in slavery. Undergirded us in peonage and coming out of it. Undergirded us in owning our farms and belongings. Undergirds our intellectual life.

That's the only way we get to the new day that we really hope for. That's why nonviolence becomes tremendously important. It has to be a spiritual thing.

You Can Move toward Danger

First came the darkness. Slavery.

My great-great-grandfather Al Sampson on my mother's side was born into slavery. He toiled in farming country in Howard County, Missouri, in the middle of the state about a hundred and fifty miles west of St. Louis.

He then left slavery to join the Union Army. After the Civil War was over, he went back to Howard County and began farming. A proud man, he refused to keep the name of the murderer who had owned him. (I refuse to call those who owned slaves, "masters.") Instead, he adopted his mother's maiden name, Woods.

My great-great-grandfather wasn't the only proud one in his family. Growing up I heard stories of two sisters on my mother's side. Apparently they were large women who wouldn't allow themselves to be pushed around . . . by anyone. They told their owners that there were certain things that they were going to do and certain things they weren't going to do. And that was that. We still tell that story because it speaks of independence.

After the Civil War, my ancestors were farmers and teachers in Missouri. My great-grandfather David E. Woods on my mother's side was, for a time, the principal of an all-Black school in Missouri. But he was fired because he started teaching the students algebra. The elders on the all-White school board couldn't do algebra themselves, so they weren't going to allow Black children versed in abstractions and equations to upstage them.

I should add here that he was alive when I was a child. Curious kid that I was, I would ask him about slavery. Having been freed when he was pretty young, he didn't have much to say. That didn't stop me. I thought if I could hypnotize him, the memories would come back. So I learned hypnosis. Never used it, though, because I heard a person put under might stay lodged in the past, and I certainly didn't want that to happen

My father, Robert Cordie Vivian (my middle name is spelled Cordy), and my mother, Elizabeth Euzetta Tindell, were married in 1919. When I was born on July 30, 1924, my father was farming in Howard County. Unfortunately, when the Depression came, we lost our land. My parents split up, and my mother, my maternal grandmother Annie Woods Tindell, and I moved into a house in nearby Boonville, Missouri.

My grandmother, who had the greatest influence on my life, was also divorced. Divorce was not uncommon in the Black or White communities during these years. Men couldn't take what happened in the Depression regardless of their race. No matter what color, everyone was scrambling to get the same food that President Hoover sent out on the weekend.

Boonville has its own rich history. Located near the easternmost point of the Sante Fe Trail and on the Missouri River, it was settled in the early nineteenth century by two of Daniel Boone's sons, who were in the salt business. During the Civil War, the town was important because it was on the route of the Missouri Pacific Railroad. The Battle of Boonville took place early in the conflict, in July 1861. The Union won that. But as the war progressed, the town was held by North and South at different times.

When we moved into Boonville, the population was about 6,500, up almost 40 percent since 1920, thanks to all the farm failures. We lived in a wood-framed house on Water Street. The property ran down a hill to the railroad tracks along the Missouri River. When the long freight trains rolled by, my grandmother would sit me in an upstairs window and make me learn my numbers by counting boxcars. Sometimes there were two hundred or more.

Later, I'll relate how I tried not to back away from sheriffs and private citizens alike wishing to do harm to me and those I led. It's not an exaggeration to suggest that some of that confidence—some might call it foolhardiness!—had its origins in Boonville.

Because of how the shadows fell on Water Street, it was often dark between the houses. One day when I was four or five, I ran around the side of our house, and there, by a walnut tree and a grapevine, I saw a ghost. I moved right toward it. Next thing I knew, I was standing in front of it. And reaching for it! *God, I hope it's not really a ghost,* I thought.

Instead of running away, I kept reaching until I grabbed that ghost's sheets. Or, I should say, the sheets my mother had hung up outside to dry. My imagination had taken hold of me, but I learned an important lesson that served me well in facing the likes of Sheriff Jim Clark in Selma thirty-five years later: *You can move toward danger. You don't have to be afraid.*

AFTER THE DARKNESS OF slavery came education.

That was the number one priority of my mother and grandmother. From the time I was born, they were determined that I would go to college. My grandmother's brother had graduated from Lincoln College, a historically Black land-grant institution that opened in Jefferson City, Missouri, shortly after the end of the Civil War. While my grandmother always regretted that she didn't have the opportunity to go to college, she never stopped educating herself . . . or me. She had me reading and doing mathematics at a third-grade level before I ever set foot in a school.

I have an early memory of playing marbles in the house on Water Street and looking up at my grandmother's impressive bookcase. One particular book caught my eye, *The Black Man: His Antecedents, His Genius, and His Achievements* by William Wells Brown. When I asked my grandmother about it, she explained that the book was about "race men. Men of mark. They made their mark in life despite the poverty and racism they faced." (I've been asked many times when I first realized that our blackness put us in a different position in the country. I always answer, "When I was born!" It's impossible not to know.)

Brown, a fugitive slave and abolitionist who traveled the world, published the book in 1863, two years before the Thirteenth Amendment abolished slavery. When I began collecting African American works, this was one of my first acquisitions. In its Preface, Brown wrote: "If this work shall aid in vindicating the Negro's character, and show that he is endowed with those intellectual and amiable qualities which adorn and dignify human nature, it will meet the most sanguine hopes of the writer."

The writer's hopes were more than realized. The book tells the stories of more than forty Black men *and* women who indeed made their marks. The names of some—Frederick Douglass and Crispus Attucks, for example—are familiar. But other heroes profiled—Phillis Wheatley, the first published African American female poet, and Joseph Cinqué, who led the revolt on the Spanish slave ship *La Amistad*—are not so well known, particularly outside the Black community.

I do not mean to leave my mother out of this story. Having married at age eighteen, she did not attend college. But she, too, valued education. She was a stoic person, very loving without showing it. Not quick to compliment, but never negative. She never said a bad word about my father.

Religion was just as important to my grandmother as education. My own sense of faith was born from going with her to Church of God the Christ in Boonville. I loved the church from the earliest age. How much? One Sunday when I was five, my grandmother told me I had to stay home from services. I was so disappointed that I ran out of the house and lay in a rut in the road. I was going to let the cars run over me if I couldn't go to church.

Why such passion? There was more life going on at God the Christ than any other place. There were all kinds of people—at least all kinds of Black people; the church was segregated like just about everything else in town. Our congregation sang loud and clear and didn't mind letting you know. They witnessed. This was different and more engaging than anything I had experienced. I don't think you can understand African American history without talking about religious life. In fact I don't think you can understand any group that has been enslaved without talking about faith in God. Case in point: Moses and the Jewish people.

When you have a grandmother as religious as mine, you know you are going to be taken care of. And most folks in the African American community had our kind of faith. We believed that somehow God was going to take care of us. We had to believe—because there sure wasn't much else in the country that said we should survive. Even though America was a democracy, we knew it wasn't a democracy for us; it was supposed to be a Christian culture, but it wasn't.

Ironically, the saving grace for us was that Blacks and Whites weren't in the same church. With few exceptions, Whites didn't want us praying with them. And for Southern Whites in particular, the church wasn't really God's, it was theirs. By having our own churches, we could have our faith without any people who opposed the movement telling us we had to obey them. Regardless of our particular denominations, we all became one faith. We were Christians, and it was God who would save us from the terrible conditions we endured. It's no surprise that the leadership in the civil rights movement came out of the church.

IT'S FAIR TO SAY that when I was about five-and-a-half, the church changed my life forever. Not, however, in the way you might think. I had no vision. I heard no voices. But there was a fire. Here's what happened. There was a couple down the street from us who had what was called a common-law marriage. This was not unusual in those days. Many men and women weren't formally married, but they had been together so long that their unions were considered legal. One night, the husband got angry and beat his wife so badly that she ran out into the cold.

This is where the church comes in. My grandmother knew the woman from God the Christ, and, believing in the teachings of Jesus, she took our neighbor into our house. Not long after that, the husband broke into our basement in the middle of the night, found the coal and wood bin, and set fire to the house.

I was asleep in my bedroom, directly above the basement, when the man did his dirty work. I heard someone call my name, jumped up, and saw that the front door was open. But for some reason I didn't understand what was happening. I laughed and got back in bed. Then I heard my grandmother calling my name again. This time I jumped up, saw smoke, and ran outside through that open door. My grandmother was in the middle of the street, being restrained by firemen who wouldn't let her go back into the house to rescue me. Within ten or fifteen minutes, the bedroom I had just escaped fell into the basement and was consumed by the fire.

Since the house was a total loss, we had to move. Rather than stay in segregated Boonville, my mother and grandmother thought life would be better if we moved to Illinois. They picked the town of Macomb for two reasons. First, its public schools were not segregated. And second, it was home to a university—Western Illinois (WIU). "No matter what happens, you'll be able to go to college here," my grandmother told me. This was rather optimistic, as I hadn't entered the first grade yet. But as I've said, my grandmother was a smart woman.

MACOMB, POPULATION 8,500 IN those days, is about 215 miles northeast of Boonville, 70 miles southwest of Peoria, and 245 miles southwest of Chicago. It was settled by veterans of the War of 1812. The railroad came through in 1855, and in 1899 Western Illinois State Normal School, the predecessor to WIU, opened its doors.

Allow me to digress here for a moment. Friends, I was made in western Illinois. I have traveled all over this country and a good part of the world. When asked where I am from, I reply, "Illinois." My questioners invariably follow up: "Oh, Chicago?"

When I tell them Macomb, they are startled that African Americans lived in western Illinois. I assure them that outside of Chicago there is indeed a place called Illinois! Then I become the object of curiosity, and they ask, "Did it affect you?" It is asked in a way that assumes I had to overcome my life in western Illinois.

I simply smile, but in my head and under my breastplate there is a rush of positive thoughts and good feelings. Even the negatives in my lifetime proved to be of great value. At the same time that my time in Macomb taught me to live in a racist society, it also taught me how good people can be, regardless of race. It also taught me that money was not a determiner of worth, again, regardless of race. However, it hurt to see people like me and others with so much talent not having a chance to use it.

The big bands came to the Tri Cities of Rock Island and over into Davenport and Fort Madison, Iowa. All the African American population of western Illinois met there. We could not go to dances in Macomb, even for Cab Calloway's band.

There were other places we could not go as well. When I won the county marble contest and it was announced that the regional was to be held in Beardstown, my mother would not allow me to go for fear; rightly so, of bodily harm. Yet one of the finest people I ever met was Churchill from Rushville, Illinois, a competitor in the high jump.

Now, back to 1930.

My mother, my grandmother, and I settled into a modest house a few blocks from the railroad tracks on Adams Street in what can generously be described as the poor side of town, income-wise. I began first grade in the middle of the school year at Lincoln Elementary, a few blocks away. Lincoln was not segregated, but there were only a handful of Black students in the entire school.

(About this time my mother married a local White businessman of what I believe was German ancestry, Leroy Huff. She became pregnant, but the baby was stillborn. My stepfather was a good guy, but that marriage, too, would eventually end in divorce—in part, I'm sad to say, because of me. I could be rambunctious, and sometimes my bad behavior warranted punishment. My mom, however, would not allow Mr. Huff to discipline me. This caused a great deal of friction between them.)

Because my classmates at Lincoln had been together since September, friendships had already been established. My mother liked to dress me up like I was rich—in knickers and colorful socks. This was not the best way to make a first impression on classmates who did not dress like they were rich. I soon had a bullseye on my back.

A ruffian named Theodore—the only other Black kid in our class—led a "gang" of first-graders, the rest of whom were White. We were dismissed each day alphabetically, so as a "V-for-Vivian," I was one of the last to leave. By that time, Theodore and his crew would often be waiting for me in front of the school. I wasn't looking for a fight, and I was smart enough to outthink my tormenters, so I would leave via the back door, cross the large schoolyard, run to the railroad tracks, and then head home safely.

That strategy worked until I had to stay after school one day. Theodore and his pals had figured out my route by then. They hid themselves behind some rocks and sand along the railroad tracks and waited. As I passed by, Theodore told one of his guys to get me. I may not have been looking for a fight, but I wasn't afraid. I beat the kid up. And I beat up the next kid Theodore sent out too. Unsure how many more attackers I could handle, I challenged Theodore to come out himself and get this over with once and for all. As I learned when I got older, a lot of bullies are all show and no go. Theodore, whose father was the minister at our new church, wanted none of me. He called the kids off, then threatened that they'd get me another time. At school the next day, I made it clear that if anyone wanted to fight me, they should come forward now. Nobody did, and that was the end of that.

This was an important learning experience in several ways. I learned not only about the hollowness of a bully's threats, but also about the senselessness of being a bully. You see, I started acting like Theodore. The story of the fight had spread quickly, so when some kids on the playground looked at me, I snarled, "Is there something you don't like?" I still remember that, because the schoolboy who was saying that wasn't the real me. I didn't like how I was acting, but I felt the need to get the message out that if necessary I'd beat up any challenger.

I want to make it clear that while I was good with my fists, I didn't go around looking for fights. I do recall a few more, however. In third grade, I went at it with Frank Thompson, a big blond classmate. We had quite a battle after school in an alley across from the school. And then—after he'd knocked me against a garage and I'd knocked him into a cinder heap—we quit and decided to be friends. First thing we did was walk down the alley to a small store and buy a bag of Our Advertiser RYO (as in roll your own) cigarette tobacco. It wasn't as fine as Bull Durham tobacco, but it cost half as much—only a nickel.

Yes, I smoked when I was in third grade; most everybody did, and I wasn't going to be left out. Frank and I divided the bag, and I went home and hid my share in a flashlight. I had gone from being a religious and God-fearing five-year-old to being an eight-year-old who rolled his own cigarettes. I still went to church with my grandmother, but I confess that my commitment was nothing like it had been in Boonville. (My grandmother and mother didn't know about my smoking or fighting until I was almost out of high school. I vowed to give up cigarettes, but that was about the hardest thing I'd ever had to do. I remember stopping one day in the middle of the street and praying for the strength to quit.)

For the rest of our time at Lincoln, Frank Thompson and I became enforcers of a kind of code that said, "You don't pick on anyone smaller than you are." Violators of that code had to deal with us.

In fourth grade, I had two memorable confrontations. I relate them to you because they're instructive in showing how I gradually came to embrace nonviolence as the righteous course of action.

Confrontation Number One began when one of my White classmates used the N-word. I couldn't tolerate that, so I hunted him down. Hands in my pocket, I egged him on until he moved his fists toward me. Before he could land a blow, I hit him in the eye. Fight over. I felt kind of bad about this because my opponent was probably using language to hurt others because he himself was from the poorest of the poor families in town and was mistreated by his parents at home and teachers at school. Still, at that time, I wasn't going to let anyone get away with such a horrendous slur.

Confrontation Number Two could have had the same outcome, but didn't. It started when a White classmate named Eugene gave me a black-faced Valentine containing several racial stereotypes and epithets—a conscious insult as unconscionable as using the N-word. When I got it, I turned around and pointed at him to let him know I was going to get him after school. True to my word, I ran after Eugene and caught him by the railroad tracks. I did everything I could to make him fight. I pushed him, I cussed him, I called him every name in the book. But he just wouldn't engage.

All the kids were there because they wanted to see the fireworks. But I couldn't make Eugene fight. And therefore I couldn't bring myself to hit him. That was an epiphany. I wanted to take him apart; he had insulted me at a level that I had not experienced, and I was not going to put up with it. But I realized I couldn't hit a kid who wouldn't fight. It's not that Eugene was incapable; he was a very good athlete. He just wouldn't fight. And so neither could I.

Because we didn't fight, I initially felt that I'd lost the argument in the minds of all the kids and that I was the loser in the equation. It was only years later that I came to realize how much that experience affected me and what I actually learned from it. This was the beginning of my true understanding of nonviolence. I gradually came to see that fighting, that *any kind of violence*, is not a solution to conflicts that might arise on the playground, at a lunch counter, or on the steps of a courthouse.

A couple of years later, as sixth grade was ending, I gathered all the guys in our group together on the school fire escape. "This is gonna be the end of fighting," I told them. "When we go to junior high school, we're not gonna fight anymore."

Why? I didn't like the bullying in the first place, and I didn't like the fighting in the second place. I just thought it was about time that we grew up. We were going to junior high school. That would be a different environment, and I wanted us to live up to it.

I ENTERED MACOMB HIGH SCHOOL in the fall of 1938. As a student there, I never thought of using the term "institutional racism" to describe the place. This wasn't because such racism didn't exist. Rather, I just didn't know there was a term to describe what I experienced. One example should give you an idea of what I'm talking about.

Some context. I was a pretty popular kid, with many friends who were Black and many friends who were White. I was also involved in quite a few extracurricular activities, including the student newspaper, and was the president of several school clubs. The junior-year play was a big deal at school, and my crowd and I really wanted to be in it. For my audition, I read Langston Hughes's wonderful poem, "The Negro Speaks of Rivers." You may know it. It begins: "I've known rivers: / I've known rivers ancient as the world and older than the flow of human blood in human veins. / My soul has grown deep like the rivers."

Miss Wagner, the faculty adviser for the play, told me I had done well enough to play the lead. Then she dropped the hammer. "It's a play that only has White people," she said. "There's no part for you. But if you want to hang around and paint the sets, you can."

I know she was trying to be nice. She was aware that the cast would be made up mostly of my White friends from French class, and that even though I couldn't paint worth a lick, this was a way for me to be involved in some way. That did not remove the pain of not being on stage. And it sure didn't erase the realization that one's talents weren't as important as the color of one's skin.

Soon after being told that all the world was literally not my stage, I learned another sad truth. This one was about another unfamiliar term: "social acceptance." One of the White girls in my class told me she was quite taken by the poem and my audition. "Your voice is the color of a robin's breast," she cooed. She invited me to dinner, but said she would have to check this out with her parents. Two weeks passed. Finally, she stopped me in the hallway. "I have to tell you that I've been dodging you," she said. "My parents told me you cannot come to our house for the evening meal and that I could do nothing about that."

That one hit me in the face. My voice may have been the color of a robin's breast, but my skin was Black. And in her household, like many White households in Macomb and, of course, the rest of the United States, I was not a welcome guest.

Another White friend, Don Coghill, reinforced the point one day at school. "All of us would like to invite you to our parties, but we can't," he confessed. That shook me too. I didn't even know they were having parties, much less that they wanted to but were prohibited from inviting me. So, step by step, slight by slight, I began to see the difference between social acceptance and acceptance in everything else. I could be a club president inside the school, but once outside I couldn't even set foot in the homes of my friends.

Let me tell you one more story from my high school years. At some point during this period, I developed a goiter. The doctor who saw me said, "No meat." My grandmother followed his orders, but when she wasn't looking, I ate some bacon from the stove. Bad idea. I went into a fit. The doctor returned and settled me down.

The fallout from this? I decided I wanted to be a doctor. For some time this made me one serious student. Eventually, however, I decided I didn't want to be the guy who fixed someone up after they got cut up or shot. I wanted to be the guy who got involved in something that stopped that from ever happening.

This epiphany coincided with my involvement in a newly formed Bible study club at the high school. After joining, I began to see the scriptures in a new light and started teaching Sunday School.

AFTER GRADUATING FROM HIGH SCHOOL in 1942, I continued my education at Western Illinois. And by education I'm referring to more than what I learned from books and lectures.

When I arrived at college, I thought that poor, uneducated White people posed the greatest threat to people of color. *The more educated you were, the more tolerant, the more above-the-fray you were.* Wrong!

I began as a sociology major but switched to English because of racism in the social sciences department. The move made no difference. The chair of the English department—a Harvard man with a PhD—refused to let me join the English club, officially known as the Canterbury Club. I was a good enough writer—sports editor of the college newspaper—but I was Black.

Bad enough, right? Well, he carried it one step further. When nine or ten White English majors threatened to leave the club over this, the chairman called them in one at a time and said if they dared to quit, they would never get a job teaching anywhere in the state. (Western had been founded as a teachers' college. Many of the students aspired to teach. And many of these would-be teachers were the sons or daughters of teachers who had made financial sacrifices for their kids. My supporters wanted to do the right thing, but they couldn't afford to cross the imperious, racist man unworthy of his PhD or department chairmanship.)

Of course, the chairman wasn't the only faculty member who favored White students over Black ones. To help pay for my tuition, I periodically helped classmates write papers. These papers were often based on assignments I had previously written. Invariably, the White student would receive a full letter-grade higher than I had gotten for basically the same paper. One student received an A on the exact paper I had received a C on the previous year.

In addition to working on the school newspaper and ghostwriting student papers, I was an active member of the Inter Varsity Christian Fellowship and continued teaching Sunday School. Years later I ran into one of my students, who reminded me that I had a unique way of motivating my class. "You paid us to memorize whole chapters, like the Sermon on the Mount," he laughed.

Thanks to one of my favorite poets, I dropped out of college before graduating. Walt Whitman had written of an America I didn't know. In "Song of Myself," he wrote, "I give the sign of democracy. / By God! I will accept nothing which all cannot have their counterpart of on the same terms."

World War II was raging, and I wanted to see this America before entering the Army, which seemed inevitable. I figured I'd return to college after my service. I never did end up in the military. No tour of duty in Europe or the Pacific. Nope. After visiting New York and Chicago, I stormed the beaches of the largest city on—are you ready?—the Illinois River. Peoria, Illinois.

Another digression, please. I want to tell you that I often think of my time in Macomb and at Western. In 1987, the university gave me an honorary doctorate. What an honor it was. How far we've come. It's a special feeling to know that all these years after my time there as a student—when the head of the English department would not allow me to join the Canterbury Club—there is now a building named after poetess Gwendolyn Brooks. And yes, there is now a department of African American Studies, when a few years ago African American women were not allowed to stay in the dormitory, and so stayed in my grandmother's house instead.

I would have happily spent my life and raised a family in western Illinois, if only custom and tradition had been willing to accept me at the level of my humanity. I feel we both lost.

2

A Matter of Faith

The Lord works in mysterious ways. How else would you explain the fact that I received my calling to the ministry in 1954 in the warehouse of a mail-order catalog company that had just made a small fortune marketing a set of ceramic cherubs called "Naughty Angels"? But before I tell you about that watershed moment in my life, let's back up. It wasn't the only life-changing experience that marked my time in Peoria. I also participated in and led my first real nonviolent direct actions. And, most important of all, I met Octavia Geans, the love of my life, the remarkable woman who would be my wife for fifty-eight years until her passing in 2011.

When I arrived in Peoria, I had every intention of returning to Macomb and earning my degree. After graduation, I hoped to attend divinity school and pursue a career in the ministry. People who knew me growing up had always told me I was going to be a minister. They had witnessed my commitment to social justice and thought I had a way with words as well. They'd also seen my commitment to the church; I had tried to unite three churches in Macomb into one solid church.

At Western, I'd been selected as one of the "Hot 100"—individuals from colleges across the country offered tuition and room and board at seminaries. I had decided on Colgate Rochester, an ecumenical divinity school in upstate New York.

You may have noticed that I said I "hoped" to go to divinity school. Why "hope"? Because even though I had a full scholarship waiting for me, I felt strongly that I shouldn't go off until I received my calling directly from the Lord. Some might say I got things backwards—that one should go *before* not *after* hearing God's call. But that's not how I felt.

In Peoria, I took a job as assistant boys director at the George

Washington Carver Community Center in South Peoria. I would have relished the opportunity to write for the *Peoria Journal Star*. Remember, I had been a sports editor on the newspaper at Western, and journalism was a true love. Sadly, however, there was an unwritten rule that Blacks need not apply for such positions at the city's leading newspaper.

You've probably heard the expression, "Will it play in Peoria?" These words which originated in vaudeville days suggest that this city in central Illinois about three hours southwest of Chicago represents traditional, mainstream, American values, and if the folks there are offended by or uninterested in something, large numbers across the country will in all likelihood feel the same way.

Truth is that when I arrived, Peoria was a pretty wide-open river town. With a population of about 100,000, it was known for whiskey, gambling, and prostitution almost as much as it was known for being the headquarters of the behemoth Caterpillar Tractor Company. Fans of the late comedian (and Carver Center alum) Richard Pryor may recall his tales of growing up in his grandmother's brothel.

Peoria in the 1940s, like Macomb and other cities in the North, didn't mandate the separation of the races like its Southern counterparts. But even if segregation didn't exist above the Mason-Dixon Line *de jure* (by law), it did *de facto* (in fact). The schools were integrated, but Blacks were virtually denied the opportunity to participate in most extracurricular activities and social events, just as I had been at Macomb High a decade earlier. With one exception that I recall, the restaurants downtown would not serve African Americans. Hotels were equally segregated. Many movie theaters wouldn't sell us tickets, and those that did required that we sit in the balcony. And, as Jason Kozlowski, a professor at West Virginia University, noted in his 2012 dissertation, *Will Globalization Play in Peoria?*, "City swimming pools admitted blacks but one day per week, thus limiting recreational activities to the then dilapidated Negro (later Carver) Community Center."

In *Furious Cool: Richard Pryor and the World That Made Him*, co-authors David and Joe Henry also note: "To give Peoria its due, let it be said that Abraham Lincoln publicly denounced slavery for the first time in a speech delivered there in 1854. And the first African American ever to vote in the United States cast his vote April 4, 1870, in Peoria."

WHEN I ARRIVED, THE Carver Center occupied an old telephone switching station in an overwhelmingly Black and impoverished area in South Peoria. It was christened in 1944 but was really a continuation of an effort initiated in 1918 by the Peoria Colored Women's Aid Society.

As Scott Saul, author of *Becoming Richard Pryor*, has written:

Moral uplift and practical help were the Center's twin themes. . . . Carver became Mecca for Peoria's young blacks. It was where they took tap or modern dance lessons, learned to play in a jazz band or on a basketball team, or held talent shows and performances. Meanwhile the pinch of housing segregation of Peoria . . . meant that Carver came to serve more than the young. The Center became a magnet for adults in the neighborhood, offering a home to community organizations and later extending much-needed services like child care and health care.

In the mid-1940s, a group of us demonstrated that with hard work, ingenuity, and faith, nonviolent direct action could play in Peoria. My participation resulted from a friendship with a housemate—a recently divorced chemist named Ben Alexander. As Black men who had witnessed and experienced discrimination and exclusion our entire lives, what choice did we have but to become involved?

Ben frequently worshipped at the predominantly White West Bluff Christian Church. When the church's progressive White minister, the Reverend Barton Hunter, launched an effort to integrate Peoria's downtown, in particular its restaurants, lunch counters, and hotels, he enlisted Ben. In turn, Ben asked if I wanted to participate.

This was my stuff. After I said, "Yes," Ben explained we'd be employing the nonviolent tactics developed a few years earlier in Chicago by Jim Farmer and the Congress of Racial Equality (CORE). "Even better," I said.

Our interracial group, which included several students from nearby Bradley University, numbered about twenty. Hunter didn't care if you were black or white or blue or red. This wasn't a matter of color; it was a matter of faith.

Faith. It's what made our lives right. When you are talking about life and death, you are really talking about your religious lives. You can't separate the two. Faith inspires you to change society, not for the sake of changing society, but because that's how you think and live. You don't have to talk about it every fifteen minutes or profess who your god is every fifteen minutes either. There was no need to do so; this was the fabric of who we were.

CORE's founders recognized this. Jim Farmer was straight out of Howard University's divinity school when he, George Houser (a White Methodist minister), and Bernice Fisher (a University of Chicago student who had attended Colgate Rochester) created the organization in Chicago. Farmer later told the writer Robert Penn Warren, "I was convinced that the current approaches to the problem were not adequate and therefore was determined to use the Gandhian techniques in the battle against segregation. We wanted to add new ingredients to the struggle that was then going on."

This remarkable interview can be found in Robert Penn Warren's "Who Speaks for the Negro?" archival collection at Vanderbilt University and on the Internet. Asked by Warren if this new strategy was "opposed to the legalistic approach," Jim explained, "We saw our approach as supplementing that approach." There would be three new ingredients:

"Involvement of the people themselves, that is the rank and file, not the talented tenth . . ."

"A rejection, a repudiation of segregation. In the past, we felt, too many people had lambasted segregation verbally and had then gone ahead and allowed themselves to be segregated."

"Emphasis upon nonviolent direct action—that is, putting one's body into direct confrontation with the evil and the perpetrators of evil and accepting the consequences of one's actions."

SO WHAT EXACTLY DID we do? First we targeted Bishop's Cafeteria, one of the establishments on Main Street that, despite laws to the contrary, refused to serve Black people. Borrowing from CORE's playbook, we demonstrated outside and held sit-ins inside. We stood in line waiting to be seated and watched as Whites who came in after we did were seated immediately.

We tried a different tactic pioneered by CORE as well. White students from our group and other White members of the church would enter in groups of two and be seated without difficulty. Each couple would try to take tables for four, leaving a pair of chairs vacant.

Then those of us who were Black would enter. As expected, we would be denied service. Instead of leaving, however, we'd wait and then, according to plan, those White folks from our group would invite us join them at their tables. "These are nice people," they would tell the exasperated manager. "We'd just like to sit and talk with them."

Picture three or four White couples doing this at the same time—while the other patrons in the restaurant were watching. The manager had to make a tough decision—throw everyone out and create a spectacle or relent. Mind you, the law was on our side.

Of course, we weren't only appealing to the manager. Others in the restaurant who saw us had to do some soul-searching. *Who am I?* they had to ask. *Am I a person that doesn't want to give other human beings the opportunity to simply sit in a restaurant and eat a meal? Am I a person who allows Black people to go to war and fight and die for me but won't let them eat in the same room?*

It took months, but eventually we prevailed. We sat down with Peoria's restaurant association and struck a deal that guaranteed us service at the downtown restaurants. The proprietors of lunch counters soon followed suit.

While we accomplished this relatively modest goal, our success in no way opened up the floodgates (or the segregated establishments) in the North, much less the South. We learned important lessons about the power of nonviolent direct action, just as CORE was learning those lessons with its sit-ins in other cities. But the perfection, if you will, of such action as a technique for effecting broad change was still several years off.

The limited access to Peoria's restaurants and recreational activities was mirrored in the workplace. Kozlowski cites a 1947 study by Bradley University's sociology department showing "that roughly ninety percent of Peoria's blacks were employed in unskilled manual labor occupations such as janitors, domestics, porters, factory workers, garbage collectors, and meat packers."

This was true at the city's largest employer, Caterpillar Tractor, where virtually the only jobs open to Blacks were janitorial. We wanted the opportunity to do more than sweep floors. Newly enacted laws said we were entitled to such opportunities, but the company argued that we were unfit for jobs requiring greater responsibilities. Caterpillar's president kept saying that Blacks could not be hired for more skilled positions because they didn't come to work on time.

Fine. For a week or two a group of us brought Black employees to work at Caterpillar every day—*on time*. After that our intervention wasn't necessary. These workers saw that they were involved in one of the most important things that was ever going to happen in their lives. By showing up on time, working hard, even staying after hours, these rank-and-file men and women were demonstrating—through nonviolent direct action—that they were worthy. More than that, they were proving that the arguments used to hold back them and their brothers and sisters were hollow. They forced the company's hand. Soon, they had the opportunity to apply for and fill those positions for which they were eminently qualified.

This is the beauty of nonviolence. By being your best self you reach others at a deeper level than they thought they could be reached. And so, the truth becomes the predominant force in what you are doing.

AFTER A WHILE, I left my job at the community center and began working at Helen Gallagher-Foster House, a Peoria-based mail-order business. Why the change? For many years, I had thought about starting a newspaper. However, I quickly determined that while I might have the necessary writing and editing skills, I lacked the business and managerial experience.

Foster-Gallagher was an appealing alternative. It was a thriving enterprise, selling a wide range of home, garden, and gift items (including ceramic angels) to people of all economic levels across the country. All economic levels, but not all races. I signed on because I saw the opportunity to start a mail-order operation geared toward the African American community. The war was over now, and Blacks had more money than in the past.

Helen Gallagher and her husband Frank, a good business team, embraced the idea. They had plans for me—but so did the good Lord. His calling finally set me on a different path.

But again, before we head down that path, I want to tell you about that most-important-of-all event: my marriage to Octavia Geans. We met in Peoria in February of 1952. At that time there were not a lot of African American professionals in Peoria. The term "networking" hadn't been coined yet, but we did just that for social and professional purposes. When a Black professional came to town, we threw a little get-to-know-you party. So, when Octavia moved from Dayton, Ohio, to take a job as women and girls director at the Carver Community Center, we celebrated her arrival with such a party.

Over the course of the evening, I learned that she had grown up in Pontiac, Michigan, outside Detroit. Her parents had moved there from Arkansas. (She later found out that her great-great-great-grandfather had been somewhat of an expert on growing rice in his native Africa. Told that if he went to America and shared his knowledge he would be well cared for, he boarded a ship only to be enslaved. A sad but all-too-common story about those from whom we are descended.)

On that first night, Octavia also told me that she had a degree in social work from Eastern Michigan University and had been working in a housing project in Dayton. She had already been involved in several actions dear to my heart. She'd participated in a door-to-door voter registration effort in her hometown and imagined returning some day to run for mayor. And she had been part of a group that integrated a popular Pontiac drive-in, Ted's Trailer.

I learned something else important that night: Octavia had a birthday coming up soon. This was my opening. A few days after the party, I called her up. "We don't want you sitting around by yourself on your birthday," I said. "How 'bout I take you out?" It took a little persuasion—I wasn't a preacher yet—but she agreed. One year to the day later—on February 23, 1953—we were married. That was her birthday, the anniversary of our first date, and our wedding date. I had no excuse for forgetting!

I DON'T WANT TO leave out another milestone in my early years. Several months after moving to Peoria, I met and married Jane Amanda Lee Teague at Mt. Zion Baptist Church. I was twenty, and Jane was sixteen. In those days it wasn't that unusual for teenagers to wed. By the time I was twenty-one, we welcomed a beautiful baby girl into the world. Jo Anna, soon known as JoJo, was born November 2, 1945, and she, Jane, and I returned to Macomb so I could resume my studies at Western. (I moved back and forth between Macomb and Peoria several times between 1944 and 1954.)

To help support my new family, I also worked. I opened a shoeshine parlor in Macomb's downtown square. And I was a waiter at a local country club. I really enjoyed this, as we waiters developed a great sense of camaraderie and support for one another.

My attraction to Jane was strong, but we were at different stages of our young lives and had different goals. When JoJo was about three, Jane and I separated. The separation was amicable, but Jane moved back to Peoria, while JoJo then lived with my mother in Macomb.

Jane and I agreed that we would not divorce until one of us wanted to remarry. That finally happened when Octavia and I became engaged. After our first child, Denise, was born, she, Octavia, and JoJo joined me in Nashville, where I'd begun studies at American Baptist Theological Seminary. But when JoJo completed the fifth grade, she returned to Macomb and was raised by my mother. I'm very happy that to this day all my children are close and love one another.

IT WAS IMPORTANT FOR me to give you this family history and introduce you to Octavia before telling the story of my calling. Now that you've met her, I can finally tell you about that summon to the ministry.

I was on the warehouse floor at Helen Gallagher-Foster when the roof seemed to open up and a voice from above boomed, "I want to work for you eight or ten hours a day." That doesn't sound like the Lord is calling, does it? I was confused, but the roof kept opening and the voice kept booming, and, well, it just filled me. I looked around to see how everybody else was reacting. It was impossible not to hear that voice. Or so I thought. But everyone was just going about their regular business. Everyone but me.

Octavia and I had been married for about a year when this calling came. Of course, I wanted to share this news with her. We were a team. And now it looked like the team would be heading east to Colgate Rochester. I waited about two or three days.

Finally, I said I had something I wanted to tell her. "I've got something I want to tell you too," she said. We usually shared these stories when were in bed, and this time was no different.

"You tell me your story first," Octavia said as we lay there.

"No, baby, you tell me," I said. I could tell whatever it was, she was bursting to get it out.

"Well, we are having our first child," she said. After we celebrated that news for a while, she said, "Well, now, tell me your story."

And I said, "No, I'm not going to tell you right now."

She finally coaxed it out of me. I told her that I had my call to the ministry, but that I wasn't going because I would have to leave her in Peoria. I needed to stay and support our family.

We laid there in the darkness, and suddenly she said, "Whose faith is in question now?"

How do you answer that? Particularly when your wife is the one asking the question and you're supposed to be the person of faith.

I started to protest and then she said, "Go to the seminary. God will make it all right."

So I went to seminary.

But not in New York.

3

Is Segregation Christian?

The headline in the *Nashville Tennessean* read "Negroes Served Without Incident: Downtown Lunch Counters Open to All." Think about this: In May 1960—some 170 years after the ratification of the Constitution's Bill of Rights, almost a full century after the end of the Civil War—it was news that black-skinned people in a city that billed itself as the "Athens of South" were for the first time afforded the same basic right to sit at a lunch counter as their white-skinned counterparts. Moreover, the *Tennessean's* editors found it equally newsworthy that this historic event passed without incident. An angry White mob didn't shout epithets at the Negroes. The police didn't drag the Negroes out. The world didn't stop turning.

Calling this a historic event is not hyperbole. At the time, no cities below the Mason-Dixon Line had laws requiring restaurants and other public establishments to serve Blacks with Whites. Federal legislation denying such policies was four years away. Nashville was thus the first major city in the South to reach an agreement allowing our people to eat at lunch counters.

The victory followed several weeks of protests, sit-ins, arrests, a bombing, the largest civil rights march in the country to date, and a dramatic confrontation on the city's courthouse steps in which the brilliant, charismatic Diane Nash—then a twenty-one-year-old student—confronted Nashville's White mayor Ben West in front of some four thousand people. "Mayor, do you recommend that the lunch counters be desegregated?" she asked.

Diane was considerably calmer than a thirty-five-year-old minister who demanded that the mayor prove his commitment to integration. In his seminal book on the Nashville sit-ins, *The Children*, Pulitzer Prize-winning journalist David Halberstam wrote that this fellow "always seemed wired, quick to explode. . . . More than any of the other Nashville ministers, he seemed able to provoke the anger, both verbal and outspoken, of his adversaries. He was intense and outspoken." Halberstam added—and this will give away the identity of the minister—"C. T., his wife, Octavia, once said, in a masterpiece of understatement, gave long answers to short questions."

I'm not sure I've changed that much since way back then, so let me give you the rather long answer to how Octavia and I ended up in Nashville and became part of a movement with such luminaries as Diane, Jim Lawson, John Lewis, Bernard Lafayette, Jim Bevel, Marion Barry, Dr. Kelly Miller Smith, and so many others to demonstrate that nonviolent confrontation was effective. No less an observer than Martin Luther King Jr. called our effort "electrifying." The Nashville Movement, he said, was "the best organized and most disciplined in the Southland."

You'll recall that after getting my calling, I expected to go to Colgate Rochester. But the Lord had different plans for me, as did the pastor of my church in Peoria. He had raised money from the congregation for me to attend an institution on whose board he sat: American Baptist Theological Seminary (ABTS) in, yes, Nashville. I enrolled in 1955, living in a student dormitory before Octavia and our first child Denise—born the previous August—joined me a few months later. Our second child, our son Cordy Jr., was born shortly after they arrived. He came two months early and should have been placed in an incubator immediately. There was, however, a delay; the doctors told us they didn't have one for Black newborns. He was soon diagnosed with cerebral palsy. I can't prove it, but I believe if the doctors had immediately treated him like a White baby his condition would not have been severe. Throughout his life (he passed away at age fifty-four in 2010), he had limited use of his arms and legs.

By the time Octavia moved to Nashville, I had found a job to help pay our bills while I went to school. Actually two jobs. I served as pastor of the First Community Church and worked as an editor at the National Baptist Sunday School Publishing Board of the National Baptist Convention. As I had been an aspiring journalist, this editorial position seemed promising. Sadly, I soon resigned as a matter of principle when the board refused to publish a twenty-four-page article based on an interview that Octavia and I conducted with Martin, who was in Nashville to receive an honorary degree from Fisk.

You'd think that an interview with the minister rising to national prominence thanks to the Montgomery Bus Boycott would have generated a great deal of excitement. The fact that it didn't sheds light on the times. The board feared that publishing the words of the "radical" Dr. King might encourage someone to bomb our offices. Fine. I quit, and Octavia and I published the article on our own. You should know that the board and I had previously clashed over my desire to give greater coverage to the nonviolent protest movement that eventually would lead to the lunch counter sit-ins.

As I explained to the landmark 1987 PBS series *Eyes on the Prize,*

WITH NUMEROUS WHITE COLLEGES and publishing houses, three Black colleges—ABTS, Fisk, and Tennessee A&I (now Tennessee State)—a Black medical school—Meharry—and three major Black publishing houses, Nashville was definitely one of the best places for a Black person to live in the South.

The point is that you have religious intellectuals—not just your (typical) Southern religionist who was really a racist, though he toted his Bible. You're thinking about people who try to purify their religion and think about it. You're thinking about educators that are not simply concerned about the normal segregationist and racist policies of education through the South, but are more inclined, not necessarily purist, but more inclined to want to see the full development of education of everyone, right? Now these tendencies within the Nashville community made it a better place to live.

I then added a big "but." While Nashville may have been preferable to other cities below the Mason-Dixon Line, life wasn't necessarily that much better for the average Black person. Nashville had a vibrant downtown, but we were second-class citizens there in all respects. No matter how educated or qualified we were, we couldn't even serve as store clerks downtown. Janitor was just about the only job available.

Many White people seemed to think they were doing us a favor to allow us to be downtown. We could shop in the stores—they would take our money—but we usually had to wait for Whites to be taken care of ahead of us. We couldn't use the bathrooms or eat downtown. These restrictions were not only a source of discomfort, they were humiliating and degrading.

Imagine shopping downtown with a child who became hungry and saw other people—other White people, that is—eating at the lunch counters in the stores or restaurants on the street. You had to drag that child out and find a Black-run establishment on the edge of town that would feed you (and let you use the bathroom). Worse, you had to answer the obvious question: "Why can't I eat there?"

I can report firsthand that this atmosphere extended to public transportation. Students of the civil rights movement know the story of the Montgomery Bus Boycott that began in late 1955 after Rosa Parks was told to move to the back of the bus merely because she was black. The boycott ended about a year later after the U.S. Supreme Court affirmed a lower-court ruling in favor of those like Rosa who had brought a lawsuit challenging the system. The case, *Browder v. Gayle*, held that Montgomery's and Alabama's enforced segregation on intrastate public transportation violated the Fourteenth Amendment's Equal Protection Clause.

About the time that the Supreme Court ruled in 1956, I climbed aboard a bus operated by Nashville's Transit Authority. Half the seats were filled, and I took a position near the front. The bus driver told me to go to the back—after all, that was the custom, if not the law, in those days. I refused to move. As Halberstam might have observed: My actions "provoked anger." After a heated argument, the driver ordered everyone off the bus, except me. He then drove me to the police station.

Believe it or not, the police did not know what the city's official policy was. They called city hall and were told that post-*Browder*, Nashville was changing its rules regarding the segregation of public transportation.

Henceforth, Blacks would not be required to take a back seat to our White brothers and sisters.

SPEAKING OF BROTHERS AND SISTERS, let me tell you about the ABTS and my remarkable fellow students and activists and our efforts during my years in Nashville. Some history about the Seminary first: It was founded in 1924 as a school to educate Black Baptists, funded in part by the city's (all-White) Commercial Club. In addition to studying for bachelor of theology or bachelor of religious education degrees, students were encouraged to do service in the community—ministering at a home for the aged, a detention home for African American girls, Meharry Medical College and Hospital, or the Nashville jail.

The Reverend Kelly Miller Smith, one of the most important figures in my life, joined the Seminary's board in 1954, when he was thirty-four years old. His name may not be as familiar to you as that of some other movement leaders, but it should be. In the mid 1950s, Ebony magazine listed him as one of the country's ten "Great Negro Preachers."

After receiving a master's from Howard's divinity school as World War II was ending, Kelly had returned to his native Mississippi to pastor a church in Vicksburg. He had then served as a college educator before moving to Nashville in 1951 to pastor at what was then called First Baptist Colored Church. John Lewis, whom you no doubt have heard of, would remember: "Students and faculty from the surrounding universities, doctors, lawyers, private businessmen and -women all filled the church's old wooden pews each Sunday to hear the words of one of the most impressive speakers I had ever listened to, the Reverend Kelly Miller Smith."

Kelly's reach extended far beyond his church. He was an integral part of a small group that sued Nashville to integrate its schools after the landmark 1954 Brown v. Board of Education decision. As president of the local NAACP chapter in 1956, he led a voter registration drive that added five thousand African Americans to the voting rolls. He taught at ABTS. And together with yours truly, he organized the first regional chapter of the Southern Christian Leadership Conference, the Nashville Christian Leadership Conference (NCLC), in 1958.

Our "Statement of Purpose and Principles" read: "If we are to see the real downfall of segregation and discrimination it will be because of a disciplined Negro Christian movement which breaks the antiquated methods of resolving our fears and tensions and dramatically applies the gospel we profess."

After forming NCLC, the question on the table was: Now what are we going to do? Kelly moved the ball forward by bringing in another movement giant whom everyone should know about, Jim Lawson. Soon we determined that our efforts should be directed at desegregating downtown Nashville, beginning with the lunch counters.

Why lunch counters? As I mentioned, Blacks could shop in downtown stores, but we could not eat at the lunch counters. We could, however, *attempt* to get service; the counters were readily accessible. Eating is a basic need, right? So demonstrating that such a basic need can be denied to a person because of his or her race provides a graphic illustration of injustice.

Jim Lawson. Although he was a few years younger than I was, he'd already done a lot by the time we met. Raised Methodist in Ohio, he followed in his father's and grandfather's footsteps and got his ministry license while still in high school. And before he had graduated from college, he had served a year in prison for refusing to serve in the Army after being drafted. After finally graduating, he was involved with two storied civil rights organizations, the Fellowship of Reconciliation (FOR) and CORE. Then it was off to India as a Methodist missionary. While there, Jim studied satyagraha, the form of nonviolent resistance advocated by Gandhi.

I will not attempt to summarize all of Gandhi's teachings here. I will tell you that in a 1925 article, "Pre-requisites for Satyagraha," he wrote that "Only when people have proved their active loyalty by obeying the many laws of the State [do] they acquire the right of Civil Disobedience." He added that those employing satyagraha must tolerate these laws, even when they are inconvenient; be willing to undergo suffering, loss of property; and endure the suffering that might be inflicted on family and friends.

Back in the U.S. in 1955, Jim enrolled at Oberlin College in Ohio to get an advanced degree in theology. A professor introduced him to another young proponent of nonviolence, one Martin Luther King Jr.

Martin, knowing a good man when he saw one, encouraged Jim to bring his teachings to the South. And so it was that Jim ended up in Nashville in 1958 as a graduate student at Vanderbilt (one of only a handful of enrolled Blacks, as the school had yet to admit Black undergraduates), a director for CORE, and the leader of workshops that trained students and others in nonviolent resistance. Kelly Smith also knew a good man when he saw one, and soon Jim was teaching nonviolent resistance to a group of us at SCLC/NCLC.

IN THE WORKSHOPS, WHICH began in late March of 1958, we simulated attempts to integrate venues that were segregated. Jim stressed that if/when confrontation arose, we should respond with love and compassion.

Through these workshops we came to understand the philosophy behind the great religious imperatives so important in terms of understanding people. At the same time we learned the tactics and techniques of nonviolent action. We learned how to take blows, how to resist fighting back when spit upon or when cigarettes were put out on us. Yes, cigarettes! We learned to respond with dignity and love because that was the righteous thing to do and the best way to realize the goals of our continuing struggle for respect and equality.

We actually practiced how to take these blows by knocking each other around. I remember an exercise where someone was instructed to put out a cigarette on one of the participating ministers. An ash fell and burned a hole in the brother's pants. He held his tongue and fists with his oppressor, but he did tell us that we'd have to buy him a new suit!

What Jim and Martin and the nonviolent movement they inspired did for Black people is that for the first time we could say, "No." If we didn't like something, we could go demonstrate. It made life miserable for both Blacks and Whites, but there was one big difference: we were happy to be miserable.

I should add here that Jim and his wife Dorothy ended up in an apartment across the street from us. Dorothy would often take our son with cerebral palsy to his special school because it was near where she worked. That deepened our friendship.

Our small crew soon expanded. Jim believed—and we agreed—that any effort to effect change needed the energy (and numbers) that local students could provide. Kelly and I had contacts at ABTS. Jim had contacts at Fisk and Vanderbilt. Kelly also had a strong relationship with Meharry. Tennessee A&I was also a prime source. And so the Nashville Student Movement was born.

The names of that movement's leaders are familiar to students of history. Lewis, Lafayette, and Bevel came from ABTS. Barry and Nash came from Fisk. This calls to mind a lyric from the recent wildly successful, award-winning Broadway musical by Lin-Manuel Miranda, *Hamilton*. In the song "My Shot," Alexander Hamilton marvels that so many committed thinkers and revolutionaries have all ended up in the same place at the same time: "Let's hatch a plot blacker than the kettle callin' the pot / What are the odds the gods would put us all in one spot," he sings. The same can be said of Nashville 185 years later.

You can read about all of the Nashville heroes in any number of books, but allow me to tell you a little bit more about Diane, who rightfully came to lead the student movement.

Unlike almost all of the rest of us, Diane was raised Catholic. She grew up in a middle-class family in Chicago. She was beautiful (a participant in the Miss Illinois competition) and, much more important, smart and fearless. She began college in Washington, D.C., at Howard but transferred to Fisk after one year. Moving to the South after all those years in the North was a shock. We did not have the opportunity to speak with her for this book, but we do have excerpts from her interview with the makers of *Eyes on the Prize*:

I heard about the Little Rock story, on the radio. And Autherine Lucy. I remember the Emmett Till situation really keenly; in fact, even now I have a good image of that picture that appeared in *Jet* magazine of him. And they made an impression. However, I had never traveled to the South at that time. And I didn't have an emotional relationship to segregation. I understood the facts and the stories, but there was not an emotional relationship. When I actually went south, and actually saw signs that said

"White" and "Colored," and I actually could not drink out of that water fountain or go to that ladies' room, I had a real emotional reaction.

Diane went on to describe her outrage when on a date at the Tennessee State Fair she saw separate ladies' rooms. "My goodness, I came to college to grow and expand, and here I am shut in. And in Chicago, I had had access, at least, to public accommodations and lunch counters and what have you. So my response was, *Who's trying to change it, change these things?*"

To her great disappointment, the answer was: *hardly anyone.* "I remember getting almost depressed because I encountered what I thought was so much apathy. Many of the students were saying, 'Why are you concerned about that?' You know, they were not interested in trying to effect some kind of change." Finally, Diane met a White Fisk student named Paul Laprad who told her about Jim Lawson's nonviolence workshops.

Interestingly, John Lewis was almost the exact opposite of Diane in terms of background. He came to Nashville from the cotton fields of a rural area near Troy, Alabama. The racism of the South was not new to him as it was to Diane. Jim Bevel was a kind of combination of these two, having grown up in both Cleveland, Mississippi, and Cleveland, Ohio. But despite all of our different backgrounds, we shared a commitment to nonviolence.

Step One. Pre-protest persuasion. We attempted to convince the major department stores to integrate their lunch counters before we need demonstrate. In November 1959, we met with Fred Harvey, the owner of Harvey's, and John Sloan, owner of Cain-Sloan. In addition to making a moral argument, we said that opening up the counters would open up a whole new stream of revenue. The two men countered that the number

Once our band of older activists, ministers, and students coalesced, we set about very deliberately to integrate downtown Nashville. Lunch counters first. Then the rest of the dominos would fall, we hoped. All's well that ends well, but it didn't go exactly as planned.

of White customers they would lose would be greater than the number of Black customers they could gain.

Step Two. Test runs. A handful of students went into Harvey's in late November and Cain-Sloan in early December. They bought a few things in the stores and then made their way to the lunch counters . . . where they were denied service (politely at Harvey's, far from politely at Cain-Sloan).

Step Three. Agree to finalize sit-in plans after the students return from holiday break. But then, on February 1, 1960, the unexpected happened. Before our plans were finalized, four Black students from North Carolina A&T staged a sit-in after they were denied food service at Woolworth's in Greensboro. By February 4, their protesting number had grown to three hundred. Two days later, some one thousand protestors and counter-protestors were at the store. Over the next week, the sit-in movement spread quickly to other Southern cities. Jim Lawson was in touch with those in the know about Greensboro. It was inevitable that we'd take action. The only question was when.

Step Four. Action. As Taylor Branch reports so well in *Parting the Waters*, on Friday, February 12:

Lawson presided over what turned out to be the first mass meeting of the sit-in movement. About five hundred new volunteers crowded into the First Baptist Church along with the seventy-five veterans of the nonviolence workshops.

Jim argued that we should delay the sit-in until those new to the cause had received training and we had raised more money for a bail fund. The students were understandably impatient, so Jim gave them a crash course on how to respond. Branch continues:

He told the crowd how to behave in the face of one hundred possible emergencies, how to avoid violating the loitering laws, how to move to and from the lunch counters in orderly shifts, how to fill the seats of students who need to go to the bathroom, even how to dress: stocking and heels for the women, coats and ties for the fellows.

Friends, a lot of thought went into these protests. And, when five hundred folks showed up at First Baptist the next morning, the Nashville sit-ins were launched.

SOME THOUGHTS ABOUT MOVEMENTS: If you're in the minority, you need a movement, and if the people won't move, you can't have a movement. Martin was special because he got people to move and, therefore, he started a movement. If they hadn't moved, he could have talked behind the pulpit forever, but nothing would have actually been accomplished.

Movements need more than a justifiable anger. There needs to be strategy and a goal. What you want for yourself and your children and the next generation is more important than having some bad feelings. That is why we were able to enact nonviolent direct action as opposed to swinging back. You have to ask: *What are you willing to commit to in order to make something happen?* And then once the commitment is there the training begins.

Okay. That sermon is over! Here's a timeline of the Nashville sit-ins, which were carried out by a committed group that, considering the circumstances, we had trained to the best of our abilities.

- Saturday, February 13, 1960. About 125 students, most of them Black, seek and are denied service at lunch counters at the S. H. Kress, Woolworth's, and McClellan establishments. The students sit in the stores for about two hours and then depart.

- Monday, February 15, 1960. As Halberstam would later report in *The Children*, the Baptist Ministers Conference, which represented about eighty congregations, threw its support behind the movement. Black religious leaders urged citizens of all colors to boycott stores that engaged in segregation.

- Thursday, February 18, 1960. Upward of eighty students are denied service at four different stores. They sit for a while, then leave without incident.

- Saturday, February 20, 1960. About 350 sit-in at several stores for about three hours. Here's Diane's *Eyes on the Prize* recollection:

The sit-ins were really highly charged, emotionally. I'm thinking of one in particular where, in our nonviolent workshops, we had decided to be respectful to the opposition and try to keep issues geared towards desegregation, not get sidetracked. And the first sit-in we had was really funny because the waitresses were nervous. And they must have dropped $2,000 worth of dishes that day. I mean, literally, it was almost a cartoon. I can remember one in particular, she was so nervous. She picked up dishes and she dropped one, and she'd pick up another one, and she'd drop it and another. It was really funny, and we were sitting there trying not to laugh, because we thought that laughing would be insulting and we didn't want to create that kind of atmosphere. At the same time, we were scared to death.

- Saturday, February 27, 1960. Push comes to shove, literally. Whites attack those students sitting in at two stores. By the time the police get there, those who did the beating are gone. "Okay, you nigras, get up and leave," say the cops. When the students—eighty-one in all—refuse the police order to leave, they are arrested on charges of loitering and disorderly conduct. "We all got up and marched to the wagon," Diane recalled.

Strategy and tactics, right? One group of students was arrested, but then a second wave took their place at the lunch counters. And when that group was arrested, in came a third wave. Said Diane:

No matter what they did and how many they arrested, there was still a lunch counter full of students, there. And it was interesting to watch their response, which was really, really surprised. They didn't quite know how to act, and pretty soon it just got to be a problem for them.

The White people at the counters began to leave or stiffen as the Black students came to sit-in. Sometimes, a person might smile out of shock more than anything else. But by-and-large it was a buildup of disdain, of not knowing what to do. And the normal Southern reaction at this point was to attack, to beat any Black. When more and more Blacks came in and sat down at the counters, the management, the waiters, and the waitresses didn't know what to do. Eventually they tried to close the lunch counters when we came in.

When they realized we were coming back every day, those opposing us changed their response. The young thuggish types in town, the Klan types in the city, began to frequent the lunch counters where we were sitting in. That's when our training proved to be most helpful—because they began to attack, put out cigarettes on people, pull people off their stools and beat them, and pour things on people. Our students were ready, and they sat there. They were prepared for it. Of course, when we were not defeated by these attacks, the police entered the picture.

Our efforts began to resonate in the larger Black community after the police started putting people in jail. Folks came forward to put up their houses as bail. A mass meeting started on a large scale. People filled the churches, whatever church we would be in—largely First Baptist but any number of those six ministers that were originally in on things. Now the movement was cooking.

This is important: The city made all the mistakes that people normally make in response to a nonviolent movement. They arrested Jim Lawson at a workshop at First Baptist and didn't really have a reason for it. As they were taking Jim out, his arm behind his back, the sign at First Baptist said, "Forgive them, Father." This made for a provocative photograph in the newspapers.

Another mistake: After putting our young people behind bars for demonstrating, the city sent them out in the snow to shovel sidewalks. Few of the students had coats, as it had been considerably warmer when they'd been arrested. The optics were not good—angering the city and further motivating the movement. Instead of being a stigma, jail became a badge of courage, a means by which you could be liberated and free. As I told *Eyes on the Prize*: "One had to pass through the jails into a promised land. Society had to be turned upside down, to be turned right side up, the new definition."

You may be wondering how the parents of these students reacted. In short: less than enthusiastically. Some feared that an arrest record would stain the future of their collegian son or daughter. Many called the university administrators and urged them to exert more control over the students. Some even pulled their kids out of school and brought them home. But in general the young protesters were undeterred. This was no less than life-changing for many of them. Would it surprise you to learn that once we started to have success, win some battles, most of the parents were really happy and thankful that their children were involved?

YOU MAY ALSO BE wondering how the powers that be in Nashville reacted. Well, even though the police represented the city and were aligned with the merchants and even the thugs, they didn't want to appear too brutal. Ah, the beauty of nonviolence. The cops wanted to stop us, but when we would not stop, then they had to address the conduct of the thugs. Why? Because the thugs brought out the darkest side of segregation in a racist society—so dark that it even shames the people who were themselves racists and who keep the system going (the government, the police, the merchants).

Of course, if you're the police, you don't have to confront thugs beating up Blacks if you arrive *after* the beatings. Invariably the police would show up late, the thugs would scatter, and we—the victims—would be arrested. Blacks across the city saw this and came to our support. Our mass meetings grew larger and larger. The support became more meaningful. More people came forward to mortgage their homes to pay for bail. *Eyes on the Prize* asked me how the White people of Nashville reacted, and I said:

The demonstrations created in many White people a fear of what was possible if Blacks united. Naturally, because of their own racism, they were afraid of anything that Blacks did, because they (Whites) were oppressors. They were always afraid of the oppressed, which created a dynamic in the city. But you see, here's where nonviolence saves us again; because no matter what they said, the oppressed were moving against the oppression with nothing in their hands with which to destroy, but something in their heart.

So, because there was nothing in our hands, they could not then react to us in the ways that the Old South normally did. They either had to accept this new loving Black man and woman, or reject themselves. Now they were caught in that kind of dilemma. Black people, on the other hand, had found a method whereby they could rejoice and yet not have any attempt to destroy the other, but only open up the society fully to everyone.

- Monday, February 29, 1960. The trial of those arrested begins. Well over one thousand community members turn out to support the students. The lead attorney for the students is Alexander Looby, a brilliant Black man in his early sixties with an undergraduate degree from Howard and a law degree from Columbia. Originally from the West Indies, Looby had been a member of the Nashville City Council for just shy of ten years. He had also been one of the lawyers behind the movement to desegregate the Nashville school system. The judge dismissed the loitering charges, but the students were convicted of disorderly conduct and fined $50 each [about $440 today].

Said Diane Nash: "We feel that if we pay these fines we would be contributing to and supporting the injustice and immoral practices that have been performed in the arrest and conviction of the defendants." Instead, the students would serve a month in the county workhouse. This is how that snow shoveling came about.

Lawson was not a part of this group. On the day the trial started, several ministers (including me and Jim) had a meeting with Nashville's mayor, Ben West. A Vanderbilt trustee who published a local newspaper took off after Jim, referring to him as, among other things, "a flannel-mouth agitator."

This led to a meeting between Jim and Vanderbilt's top brass, who insisted he absent himself from the sit-in movement. When Jim refused, he was expelled. Within twenty-four hours he was arrested for inciting the students. The irony was not lost on us that the chancellor of Vanderbilt, Harvie Branscomb, was a theologian whose books included The Message of Jesus. (On the other hand, J. Robert Nelson, the dean of Vanderbilt's divinity school, resigned in protest over the expulsion and joined with others in paying Jim's five hundred dollar bail.)

- Thursday, March 3, 1960. Mayor West forms the Biracial Committee, a group of city leaders (including local Black college presidents, but none of the students) to address the sit-ins and the overall racial divide in Nashville.

- Tuesday, April 5, 1960. The Committee issues its recommendations. Vanilla and Oreo sections. I'm being facetious, but what I mean is the Committee recommended that stores should have two kinds of lunch counters: one for Whites only and one for Blacks and any Whites who might choose to join them. We at the NCLC said, no thank you. So did the students—quickly. So quickly that the community couldn't keep up with them. They would have meetings at six in the morning, before classes, and then again later in the day.

When Diane and the other students learned that the Biracial Committee had issued its report, they responded immediately. That report recommended that Blacks and Whites start at opposite ends of the lunch counters and fill inward. Unacceptable! We wanted to be treated as equals, wanted to be able to come to the counters and be served like our White counterparts. So the sit-ins resumed. As Diane later noted, this strategy made it difficult for those who might have supported the committee's suggestion to do so. "I loved the energy, that kind of feeling that being right gave us," Diane said.

In addition to the sit-ins, we organized what has been called an Easter Boycott of the downtown stores, though we preferred to call it an "economic withdrawal." This allowed us to show our desire to be fully integrated into the life of the city, to demonstrate many ideas of nonviolence, and to help create a reconciliation of all the forces in Nashville. Our theology taught us that those resources that God gave you could not be used to perpetuate an evil. So putting those resources in the hands of merchants who were perpetuating the evil of racism was against God, a misuse of that which was given, number one.

Along with Christmas, Easter was our most important time for buying. No matter how poor you were, everyone in the Black community had to have a brand-new outfit. You may start paying three months ahead of time for that outfit, and you may still be paying for it for three months later. The amount of money wasn't that much, but because the difference in White and Black income was so great and you had so little money for extras, you could be paying for six months.

Of course, Easter was also the time of the cross, a time of sacrifice. So surely we could sacrifice. Our people found they did not need new suits, new clothes, new shoes, new anything. As one woman said, "I looked in my closet and found I had fourteen pair of shoes, and I said, 'I am so glad for the movement 'cause I don't need to buy anything.'" I remember a number of men saying that for the first time they were solvent after Easter than they had spent for Easter inventory. The two Nashvilles system wasn't going to work anymore.

As I told *Eyes on the Prize:*

People began to put things in economic terms. Vivian Henderson, an economist at Fisk University at the time, would give weekly reports showing us that the economic withdrawal was destroying the downtown economy.* The merchants could no longer count on getting back the money that they had spent for Easter inventory. The two Nashvilles system wasn't

Everybody in that city began to realize that there needed to be a rec-onciliation—the merchants because of the money lost, people in that city because it was being interpreted in terms of the cross and it was a religious city, with all those churches. Everyone was affected from their base of values, and that made the difference. And as they were affected there, they began to interpret the movement not simply as a group of Blacks who were dissatisfied. But in terms of the evil in the society and how badly fractured we were as a city and what could happen then in terms of a vision of the possibility of a true democratic city that could fulfill their understandings of the Athens of the South that was worthy of a Parthenon.

---

* I should note that when Dr. Henderson later became the president of Clark College in Atlanta, he granted Cordy and his sisters Denise and Kira Presidential Scholar-ships. Given my salary during that time, it was not only appreciated, but necessary.

• Tuesday, April 19, 1960. A group of movement leaders—students and ministers, including myself—were to hold a morning strategy session in the Reverend Anderson's Methodist church near the Fisk campus. Before we got there—around 5:30 a.m.—most of us heard a huge explosion. We soon learned that a bomb had been thrown through the front window of Lawyer Looby's home. Fortunately no one was hurt, although the house was badly damaged. The blast was so great that 147 windows were blown out in a nearby Meharry Medical College dorm.

We knew we had to respond. Such an act demanded that the city fathers come to terms with the moral bankruptcy of existing policy—even if they didn't countenance the bombing itself. Throughout our history, we have been compelled to view such heinous deeds as opportunities; as terrible as it was, this violent act could be very useful to our nonviolent movement. How could we channel the energy we were feeling to accomplish our goal of ending segregation in the city?

We decided to mobilize students at ABTS, Fisk, Meharry, and Tennessee A&I, as well as the community at large, for a march to city hall. We prepared a statement to be read aloud when we got there. And we determined that Diane and I would speak for us.

So you see, we were prepared for this moment—didn't welcome it, but were prepared. Without doubt, this was a turning point—not just in Nashville, but in the movement itself. In many ways we'd been leading up to this without really knowing it. This would be the first major march of the modern civil rights movement.

We began the march right after lunchtime at Tennessee A&I on the city's outer limits. Bernard Lafayette, who would become a great friend for life, had done a terrific job of spreading the word there. Students came out from the lunchrooms, buildings, and dormitories as we started. The leaders of the movement were up front, so that everyone knew them. We marched three abreast. People along the way began to join us in small numbers. They knew this was serious.

When we got to 18th and Jefferson, Fisk students were waiting and fell right in. One block later, students from nearby Pearl High School joined us. Then people started coming out of their houses. Everyone was enthusiastic. The camaraderie was apparent. At the same time, there was a certain seriousness, an undeniable collective sense of purpose.

Pretty soon you could hear the feet, and then that was taken over by cars coming and joining us along the way. They moved very slowly so they could be with us as we marched. We filled Jefferson Street. Eventually our line would stretch ten full blocks.

It's a long way down Jefferson to city hall. At first there was a certain bit of singing. But as we came closer to town, we fell silent. Indeed, some of the students carried mimeographed sheets that said: "We shall let our complete silence be our only speech."

All you could hear was the sound of our feet on the street pavement. This conjured memories of what was called the Silent Protest Parade when in July 1917 ten thousand people, led by W. E. B. Du Bois and others, had marched down New York's Fifth Avenue in silence to protest lynchings in East St. Louis, Illinois, and the pervasive climate of white supremacy.

As we got closer to downtown Nashville, we passed a bare expanse that had been cleared for urban renewal. We walked by a place where there were workers out for the noon hour. White workers, and they had never seen anything like this. Four thousand people marching down the street, and all you could hear was their feet.

Those workers didn't know what to do. They moved back against the wall and simply watched. They, too, were silent—in awe of us, I think. They did not know what to do, but they knew that this was not to be stopped, this was not to be played with or to be joked with.

We had sent a telegram to Mayor Ben West saying we would be coming to city hall and that our march would be nonviolent. When we arrived at about 1:30, West was waiting for us on the steps. A forty-nine-year-old former assistant district attorney, he was more progressive than most mayors in the South. But he had not exerted the moral authority of his office to effect the desegregation that we were demanding.

I recently discovered a copy of the April 20, 1960, *Nashville Tennessean.*

The front-page story about our march was written by a twenty-six-year-old reporter for the paper just beginning what would be an illustrious career, the aforementioned David Halberstam. His description of the events is no doubt more eloquent than mine could ever be. And because he was writing contemporaneously—as opposed to almost sixty years after the fact—I trust his account more than my memory. So here are some choice excerpts of the piece, which ran under the bold headline: INTEGRATE COUNTERS—MAYOR.

Mayor Ben West told three thousand demonstrating Negroes yesterday he thought Nashville merchants should end lunch counter segregation, but the mayor standing in front of the courthouse, surrounded by a sea of Negroes which overflowed into the street added: "That's up to the store managers, of course, what they do. I can't tell a man how to run his business . . ."

The Negroes then applauded the mayor. The applause contrasted sharply with the stony silence with which the crowd had watched the mayor moments before as he exchanged heated words with several of their leaders. The sharp words came as the Reverend C. T. Vivian, Negro leader and pastor of First Community Church, read a group statement sharply critical of West for what it termed his failure to lead.

West, his hat off and his voice carrying, said: "I deny your statement and resent to the bottom of my soul the implication you have just read."

He tried to continue speaking, but Vivian shouted in his ear: "Prove it, Mayor, prove the statement is wrong."

Halberstam wrote that, "Only a third of the line had arrived when Vivian started reading the Negro statement." That statement accused the mayor of several wrongs, including failing to use the moral weight of his office to speak out against the hatemongers, being difficult to reach, and trying to slow things down until the students went home for the summer.

Then Vivian read: "Because he has failed to speak, we ask that he now consider the Christian faith he professes and the democratic rights of all our citizens and declare for our city a policy of sanity based on our common faith and our democratic principles." When Vivian finished, the Negroes burst into prolonged applause. There was no vocal cheering—just clapping of hands.

Then West spoke. First he said he deeply resented the implications of the statement. Vivian, by his side, seemed to argue with him several times. Vivian was later restrained by another Negro minister. "I intend to see that order is maintained," West said. "As God is my helper, if anything can be done to find the man who bombed my good friend Looby's home, we'll do that."

The crowd was still gathering. West was pocketed among a group of the Negro leaders. One of them, Vivian, started the questioning. He asked the mayor if segregation were moral. "No," the mayor said. "It is wrong and immoral to discriminate."

Then, Miss Nash, a Fisk junior from Chicago, took over the questioning. She asked West to use "the prestige of your office to appeal to all the citizens to stop this racial discrimination."

West answered: "I appeal to all citizens to end discrimination, to have no bigotry, no bias, no hatred."

Miss Nash asked: "Do you mean that to include lunch counters?"

West answered, "Little lady, I stopped segregation seven years ago at the airport when I first took office, and there has been no trouble there since."

But Miss Nash asked one more question: "Then mayor, do you recommend that the lunch counters be desegregated?"

That is when West answered: "Yes," turned slightly and added, "That's up to the store managers, of course."

I couldn't stay silent.

Then Vivian asked, "Do you realize that this goes deeper than the lunch counter, that it can destroy us?"

West answered: "You also have the power to destroy, I want you students to realize this . . ."

Vivian then asked: "Is segregation Christian?"

West told Vivian to look at his past record. "What a fellow does often speaks so loud you can't hear his words."

Vivian said he was not asking about the past record.

I trust the above gives you a strong sense of what happened, as well as who I was. Reading it now I can't say I disagree with Halberstam's assessment that I was "wired, quick to explode." But I have no regrets that this was my style. I am also grateful that Diane provided such a complementary style.

A postscript is required.

- Tuesday, May 10, 1960. At 3 p.m., groups of two or three Blacks, mostly students, enter six Nashville department stores and take their seats at the lunch counters—the lunch counters that had previously only been open to White patrons. Among the items they order: club steaks and hamburgers. As the *Tennessean* would report, one store official said, "There was no reaction whatsoever from our White customers."

Over the previous weekend, we had finally reached an agreement with the storeowners. It was far different from the earlier plan proposed by the Biracial Committee. Blacks would come to the counters in small groups at slack hours for several days so that integration could be introduced gradually, in a less threatening fashion, to avoid confrontation or violence.

The plan worked. And then, as John Lewis put it, we began a march through the yellow pages to integrate other public venues. (Remember, this was four full years before the U.S. Congress passed the 1964 Civil Rights Act.) The march took time. A year passed before we achieved another major milestone: integrating the downtown theaters. I remember that because the victory was celebrated with a picnic on Mother's Day in 1961—the same day that Klansmen attacked the Freedom Riders in Anniston, Alabama.

I wasn't in Anniston, but I soon was on a bus . . . and then in prison.

4

And Then They Jumped on Me

I've only had a few truly religious experiences in my life. You already have read about one of them: when I was in that warehouse in Peoria in 1955, and the Lord finally called me to the ministry. Another one, which I'll describe in a later chapter, took place in 1965 in a Selma jailhouse. Then there was the spring of 1961, when I was imprisoned with scores of fellow Freedom Riders at the infamous Parchman Farm, a.k.a. the Mississippi State Penitentiary.

First, I had to get from Nashville to Mississippi. Another timeline is in order. This one will put the Freedom Rides in context—*briefly*. My purpose here is not to tell you the complete story of that momentous undertaking. Any number of wonderful books can do that, including Taylor Branch's *Parting the Waters* and Raymond Arsenault's *Freedom Riders: 1961 and the Struggle for Racial Justice*. PBS also presented an excellent, in-depth documentary series on the subject. No, my purpose is to give you one man's personal experience.

- Thursday, May 4, 1961. Two buses—one Greyhound, one Trailways—leave Washington, D.C., for New Orleans. On board are a baker's dozen of the very first group of Freedom Riders (in the 1960s, at least) led by Jim Farmer of CORE. John Lewis, scheduled to graduate from ABTS in a few weeks, is also on board. Their goal? Force the hand of the federal government to enforce U.S. Supreme Court and Interstate Commerce Commission rulings that hold that segregated *interstate* transportation (as well as the segregation of restaurants and waiting rooms) is unconstitutional. I say force Washington's hand because the Southern states were perfectly happy to thumb their noses at the established law—without consequence.

The buses are to travel through Virginia, North Carolina, South Carolina, Georgia, Alabama, and Louisiana. A rally is planned upon their arrival on May 17. The planners have not exactly reinvented the wheel. In 1947, the Fellowship of Reconciliation and CORE had organized a similar journey to force federal enforcement following a Supreme Court ruling that Virginia's law that mandated the segregation of interstate travel violated the Equal Protection Clause.

Remember I've talked about the importance of strategy. The 1961 Freedom Riders were seven Blacks, six Whites. The Blacks deliberately sat in the front of each bus customarily (and illegally) reserved for Whites. They also violated tradition by sharing seats with their White counterparts.

- Tuesday, May 9, 1961. There have been a few arrests to date, but no violence. That changes in South Carolina. John Lewis would later remember: "My seatmate was a young White gentleman named Albert Bigelow. He was from Connecticut. Wonderful man. We arrived in a little town called Rock Hill. We got off the bus and started into a so-called White waiting room, and the moment we started through the door a group of young White men attacked us and started beating us and left us in a pool of blood. We were asked if we wanted to press charges. We said no."

- Sunday, May 14, 1961. Mother's Day finds movement members in Nashville at a picnic celebrating the first anniversary of the successful lunch counter sit-ins. But the celebratory mood quickly disappears when we receive word that the Freedom Riders have been brutally attacked in Alabama. The attacks are the result of collusion between the Klan and law enforcement officials.

Attacks Number One and Two take place near Anniston. Klan members slash the tires of the Greyhound bus and then . . . Author Arsenault offers a graphic history:

After returning to his car, which was parked a few yards behind the disabled Greyhound, Cecil "Goober" Lewallyn suddenly ran toward the bus and tossed a flaming bundle of rags through a broken window. Within seconds the bundle exploded, sending dark gray smoke throughout the bus. At first, Genevieve Hughes, seated only a few feet away from the explosion, thought the bomb-thrower was just trying to scare the Freedom Riders with a smoke bomb, but as the smoke got blacker and blacker and as flames began to engulf several of the upholstered seats, she realized that she and the other passengers were in serious trouble. Crouching down in the middle of the bus, she screamed out, "Is there any air up front?"

When no one answered, she began to panic. "Oh, my God, they're going to burn us up!" she yelled to the others, who were lost in a dense cloud of smoke. Making her way forward, she finally found an open window six rows from the front and thrust her head out, gasping for air. As she looked out, she saw the outstretched necks of Jimmy McDonald and Charlotte Devree, who had also found open windows. Seconds later, all three squeezed through the windows and dropped to the ground. Still choking from the smoke and fumes, they staggered across the street. Gazing back at the burning bus, they feared that the other passengers were still trapped inside, but they soon caught sight of several passengers who had escaped through the front door on the other side.

They were all lucky to be alive. Several members of the mob had pressed against the door screaming, "Burn them alive" and "Fry the goddamn niggers," and the Freedom Riders had been all but doomed until an exploding fuel tank convinced the mob that the whole bus was about to explode. As the frightened Whites retreated, Cowling (an undercover Alabama Highway Patrol officer on board) pried open the door, allowing the rest of the choking passengers to escape.

To escape, only to be beaten by the mob.

Later, Klan members board the Trailways bus and beat its Freedom Riders before the bus can continue its journey westward.

Attack Number Three takes place in Birmingham. With the blessing and assistance of Police Commissioner "Bull" Connor, Klansmen waiting in the Trailways bus terminal beat the Freedom Riders with baseball bats, iron pipes, and other weapons. Some Whites-only hospitals refuse to treat the injured.

Now what? The Riders decide to soldier on from Birmingham to New Orleans. U.S. Attorney General Bobby Kennedy promises protection on the ninety-mile journey to Montgomery. The bus companies, however, refuse to get on board. *Too dangerous for our drivers*, they say.

This isn't what the Riders want. On the other hand, thanks to press coverage of the terror in Alabama, they've already heightened the nation's awareness to the unfair, immoral state of affairs and, once again, have challenged government officials and White Americans to do some soul-searching. *Can you continue to look the other way?* The Riders decide to fly to New Orleans.

This brings us back to Nashville. After getting word about Anniston and Birmingham, a group of us met that evening to figure out next steps. Diane Nash led the discussion.

Should we try to resume the rides? The assembled had a variety of strongly held opinions. Some argued that, in light of what had happened in Alabama, the mission was simply too dangerous.

Acknowledging that danger, Diane made an argument that I endorsed. On *Eyes on the Prize* years later, she reflected:

If the Freedom Ride had been stopped as a result of violence, I strongly felt that the future of the movement was going to be cut short. Because the impression would have been given that whenever a movement starts, all that has to be done is that you attack it—massive violence and the Blacks would stop. And I thought that was a very dangerous thing to happen. So, under those circumstances, it was really important that the Ride continue. And again, part of the nonviolent strategy understands that when that type of negative image is directed at you, one of the important things to do is find ways to convert it to positive energy, which we were able to do as a result of continuing.

John Lewis, who had returned to Nashville after Rock Hill, remembered that night too: "A group of us in Nashville, met with the adults and told them we needed $900 to $1,000. We were going to continue the rides. We met on a Sunday night and they told us no, it would be like committing suicide. And we begged and we pleaded and finally they made a decision to make $900 available to us for ten tickets and for food along the way."

- Wednesday, May 17, 1961. The ten students leave by bus for the three-hour drive to Birmingham. When they get there, Connor arrests them. In jail, they demonstrate how freedom songs have long sustained us and can even win the day. Their singing so annoys the beefy Connor that he orders them released and driven back to the Tennessee state line.

- Saturday, May 20, 1961. Undaunted, the students had returned to Birmingham. They had attempted to ride to Montgomery the previous day, but a White mob had prevented the bus drivers from getting through the depot. After the U.S. Justice Department intervenes, Alabama Governor John Patterson agrees to provide safe passage from Birmingham to Montgomery. But the highway patrol escort departs at the Montgomery city line, all but ensuring what happens next to the group of riders, which includes Lewis and Bernard Lafayette. Local police watch as a mob waiting at the bus station reprises the brutal beatings of Mother's Day. Lewis is badly injured, while Lafayette barely escapes.

- Wednesday, May 24, 1961. A dozen "reinforcements" who have come from Nashville to Montgomery board a bus bound for Jackson, Mississippi. I'm among them, as are Jim Lawson, Jim Bevel, Bernard Lafayette, and other movement stalwarts.

There's no question danger awaits us on the road or in the bus terminals. In all likelihood, Mississippi will be as bad as or worse than Alabama. At thirty-six, I'm one of the older participants. Octavia and I now have five children. This gives me pause. But when I tell Octavia what I want to do, she says, "If you have to go, you have to go." I'm not surprised. We both had trained for this.

That's what training does. You know what you are getting into. If you're not ready, you shouldn't be there. You know what you're doing. Know the cost on both sides. By that I mean, you know the cost if you don't go. You know that all your life you've been waiting to get rid of racism, and you know that until you break it in the South, it won't be broken. So let's get it on! We had a method, and as far as I knew, it worked. I had a God who sent me.

My wife knew this too. We did this together. That's important to see. Praise the women of the movement. Our wives knew, and we did it together. Octavia had left Dayton and gone to Peoria, then Nashville. She understood that this was more than something that just happened. She understood that the God that took her from Dayton to Nashville was the same God that would take care of her whether I was there or not. She was my partner in everything I did.

None of the men who have garnered so much attention for their roles in the movement could have accomplished anything without the support, encouragement, and counsel of their spouses—who for long stretches of time were, in effect, single parents. Octavia and others—just as committed to the movement as their husbands—ran the households and raised the children, all the while worrying whether we would return in one piece, or at all. Two words: fifty-eight years.

When Taylor Branch interviewed me on film in 2011 for the Civil Rights History Project (you can find the complete interview on the Internet and at the National Museum of African American History and Culture in Washington, D.C.), I shared my memories of the Freedom Ride with him. We started with events in Montgomery.

When we got onto the bus in Montgomery, there were already White people on the front of the bus. And we had to go to the back of the bus because there was no other space. They'd put the White people on first, put them right up front, and the rest of us had to go to the back behind them. Then when we got on, the state troopers came and got the White passengers off the bus, and then filled those first three or four rows with the Alabama militia, and we started for Jackson.

When we got to the Mississippi state line, the bus stopped, and the Alabama militia got off. As we were going to the state line, there was a long trail of cars behind us. Most of them turned out to be news people. When we stopped to change so that Mississippi militia could take the place of

Alabama militia, the news people came up and asked questions.

We'd made up our minds that we were not going to have everybody do the talking, and we chose Jim Lawson to explain nonviolence to them—because that's what we wanted them to know. We had learned that what you do, no matter what the press wants, you tell them what *you* want, and they have nothing to use but what you said. So you would get your story out, regardless of what was asked. It was handled that way, but I remember the *Life* magazine front cover—or maybe it was the headline over the article—"Asking for trouble and getting it."

They didn't understand nonviolence, and nothing Jim said or anybody else said. But that's why we had the movement in the first place. That's what it was all about, because we couldn't have moved the nation without the understanding of nonviolent direct action. (Unfortunately) the news people did not get it.

When we moved on from the state line, a colonel from Mississippi got on. He undid the bus's speedometer and told the driver to go into Jackson, and boy, they just barreled into Jackson. I mean, barreled in.

All along the way, in every little town we'd come to, people were out on their porches, which is a Mississippi thing anyway. And they were out there and they'd be waving at us and so forth and they knew we were coming. They weren't saying nothing, they weren't hollering nothing, but they were all waving. And then later on as we came closer and closer to Jackson and the towns got bigger, people came right out to the edge of the road and waved.

When we got to the terminal in Jackson, everybody had to go to the bathroom. The colonel didn't want to stop for us. But we were anxious to make our stand and use the Whites-only facilities. I was the last to get off the bus because we had decided we wanted someone experienced on the back end.

I saw the police were putting our people into a wagon to go downtown as fast as they came out from going to the bathroom. Being the last one out, I came past just as they were getting ready to close the doors of the wagon. So I patted the policeman in charge on the back and said, "I'm with them." He couldn't help but smile. I think that's the first time anybody ever asked him to go to jail, right? He straightened it up and turned back around and he said, "Get in there." So I got in, and we all went to the city jail. (There was a Hinds County jail, too, but we went to the Jackson city jail.) Later Jim Farmer (the head of CORE) joined us. He was on a second bus that had left Montgomery after ours.

At this point in the interview Mr. Branch reminded me that both Bobby Kennedy and Mississippi Governor Ross Barnett were shocked to learn that there had been a second bus. We all learned later that the U.S. attorney general had made a secret deal with Barnett and John Patterson. As long as they provided protection to us while we traveled through their states, local law enforcement officials could arrest us Freedom Riders for violating their own states' segregation laws—such as using a Whites-only bathroom. Attorney General Kennedy and the governors hoped this would throw cold water on future rides. In other words, even though we were moving from state to state to force enforcement of existing laws prohibiting segregation with regard to *interstate* travel and use of facilities, Washington was willing to let states arrest us based on the patently false determination that we were engaged in *intrastate* travel.

Besides being contrary to the law of the land and, of course, the laws of human decency and respect, the plan had a critical flaw. Neither Washington nor the states realized how resilient and relentless we would be. A second bus came, and later a third, a fourth, and even more.

We were held in the jail for at least a week, probably closer to ten days. Then that city jail, as well as the county jail, became so crowded with Riders arrested from those subsequent buses, the authorities had to move us to Parchman.

Our stay at the county jail was really quite remarkable. Despite being held in several different jail cells, we conducted a Sunday service. How? We wrote up who was to do what and passed it through the bars to each other—who was opening, who was singing, who was doing everything. That kind of coordination extended beyond the Sunday service.

Back to the interview with Branch:

We set up a whole routine. I think that's very important to know, because it showed how to do nonviolent direct action. The thing that surprised (our jailers) is that (in the past) they'd always slipped food through the place where they're supposed to slip it through, but then people would fight for it, fight for their meal.

Not us. We all went and sat down in our chairs around the tables that we had, and we'd have two of our people delivering the food (that had been slipped through the bars) to us. And that just stunned them—they just didn't ever understand that we were having order. It put us in charge in a way that they didn't like. They were so used to people just wanting the food and fighting with each other over it.

This deeply impressed the black prisoners who were jail trusties. From that moment on, we could trust them. They would do things for us. They'd let you know in meaningful ways that they were on our side, and that whatever negative things they did they had to do because of the White guards. And that was very important to us because they saw that sense of dignity we had, and they understood what effect it had on the White people running the jails. . . .

I remember there was a White lieutenant type. He had something in for me. I was trying to get where he was coming from. I just couldn't understand it, so I asked Jim Bevel because he was originally from Mississippi. "What is wrong with this guy?"

And Jim laughed and he says, "You're a man."

And I said, "What the heck are you talking about?"

And he said, "He's not used to anybody Black looking him in the eye. To look him in the eye to him was almost an insult, and you never turned away, and you talked to him straight."

Hmm. I wasn't being unusual, I was just talking to him, just like you'd talk to somebody, right? And it seemed like the more we talked, the madder this guy got, and yet there was nothing in the conversation to me that would create anger under any circumstances. And Jim laughed because he was the only one that understood this White-Black relationship. We Northerners didn't.

So they wake us up the next morning very early and take us to Parchman.

Parchman Prison is one of the most vicious prisons ever. They had two burial grounds there. It's a farm-prison. It was modeled on a plantation. In fact it was probably a plantation at one time before it was the farm that they used. And they don't know how many people were killed in that thing. Because there wasn't any real formal cemetery arrangements, as much as people were just buried on top of each other as they died and as things went on.

So we get to Parchman, and the next day they start questioning us. There was a girl in the room being questioned right before me. She ends up in tears. I could hear it through the walls. And we were upset about it, but nothing to do about it. In fact, we weren't even where you could see in. We were hearing through the walls.

And I was next. Well, this (same) guy that didn't like the fact that I was looking, just looking at him and talking, he was there at Parchman. He didn't go back to the Jackson jail. He stayed at Parchman for all the questioning. When they asked me a question, I said either yes or no. And then they said, "Say sir." Fine. I wasn't there to be making an argument for anything, so I said "sir."

They asked a couple of other simple questions, and then they asked me right quick, "Do you have syphilis?" And I said, "No." And they jumped on me. We were sitting close to each other, and they jumped on me. There were about four or five of them, and they jumped on me.

Well, it was obvious that this is what the guy from Jackson had been waiting for. Out he comes with his slapjack, and he's right down on top of me. And I was just warding off blows. That caused his hand to turn, and from my angle, it was no longer an ordinary slapjack. It had edges. See, some of them are just black leather around a piece of lead. This one was embellished with figures. But it was so pretty. It was thick tan leather so that steel was inside. But it was thick and it had sharp edges, and when his hand turned, it was no longer hitting you like a slapjack would. It turned and it cut me right down the side, there.

As soon as the blood spurted out, they jumped back. I mean, they jumped back and they looked at each other. I wondered what really happened, because I didn't understand until later. I was looking at them as if to say, "What is this all about?"

No more beating, no more questioning. They had a guy take me back to the cells. So he's taking me back to the cells, and we make a turn and go down, you make a turn and go straight on into the first part of the cells, and then there was a turn there, right where a great big steel gate was.

So the guy unlocks the gate and tells me to go on in. So I start in, and I'm going into the jail, and suddenly I feel something right down the back of my neck. And it looked like a half question mark in my mind, and I saw it as red, and only occasionally do I ever dream in color, and I wasn't dreaming, and I was standing up walking and I could feel this thing, and so I stopped and I look around at him, because any time anything that you've never felt before and never had any knowledge or thought of happens to you, what you do is to turn to any human, another human being, you know, anybody that's there. So I turned around to look at him and so much as if to say, *Did you feel that?* Then I realized I was looking at a .45 or a .38, either one—I think it was a .38, actually.

I was looking into the barrel of this .38 because I was looking in his eyes, because you look to see him, you know, to ask him the question without announcing it, you know, *What did you feel? You're feeling at the* same time you're asking, and then I realized he had a gun on me, and I was looking down the barrel of it so I just kind of slumped and looked at him there. And so I look at him, and he's got this .38 on me, and I just look at him and I look him straight in the eye, looking, *What is wrong with you?* as if to say, *What kind of human being are you? You know what I mean?* I just couldn't take it in, that somebody was standing there with a gun. You're just, you're going to take two more steps and you're totally inside with all the other guys, right? Because you have to make little quick turns with all the other guys, right? Because you have to make little quick turns there. And so I look at him, and he's got this .38 on me, and I just look at him and I look him straight in the eye, looking, *What is wrong with you?*

And he's trying to make up his mind whether he's going to shoot me or not. That's obvious, and I just keep looking at him, and he decides he's not going to shoot me, so he just pulls down his gun and throws it in his holster, slams this big steel door and those big jail doors, you know, you don't forget the sound of them, right? I can't repeat it, but you don't forget the sound of it.

And then he turned around and walked straight down that long hallway, and I just kept looking until he came to that first turn going back. All this time I'm bleeding. I remember being beat like that in another place, but in that place they had doctors come. But this one, I don't remember a doctor coming at all.

So I go on in and the guys, the other prisoners, wonder what's happening and we talk. But then (a little later) the prison officials let a guy out because by that time there were more of our people all over the jail. Remember, bus after bus kept coming. It wasn't just one bus or two buses. Buses kept coming, kept coming, kept coming, and so this one White fellow that was being held with us was let out for some reason.

He was let out, and there was press that he talked to, and then Washington began to call. Afterwards I understood. What really happened is they were not supposed to beat anybody. And they beat me until I bled, right? That's what they were upset about—not the beating, but the fact that I bled.

This White guy told the press that I'd been beaten. Kennedy got it within a couple hours, and it was back on the warden. The warden was very, very fearful that he was going to be removed. We found that out later—I didn't know that—but we found that out later.

Then about that time, Kelly Miller called, and within hours he showed up. Remember, all this started early in the morning, and Kelly showed up and took me back to Nashville.

I wished I had been there all summer. I wasn't there but a week and a half, two weeks. Then the blood came out. I was saved by the blood. By the way, I used that—when we got back to Nashville. When Kelly brought us back to Nashville, we went to a mass meeting, and that's what I used as text. That there is no redemption of sin without the shedding of blood. . . .

Being a Freedom Rider has been a large part of my understanding of my identity. But the major one for me internally is the one where I got that feel down the back of my head and that this guy wanted to shoot me and didn't. Now, that to me is the deepest piece. It was as though I was warned. Parchman is a place where they kill anybody black any time they want to, right?

We were the only two there because whatever the prisoners said wouldn't have made a difference; we couldn't even see them. It's the mystery of that. I feel something that causes me to turn around, and the guy's got the gun on my head. And when he invited me in—it was almost like he was doing me a favor inviting me in—and then suddenly when I feel this red—I can see red, right—down the back of my head, and I turn around and there's that gun.

This was the religious experience I talked about at the beginning of this chapter.

When I was interviewed by the National Visionary Leadership Project about my life and about the Freedom Rides in particular, I added this:

After I go back to my cell and I'm lying there, that was the test of non-violence, Because this guard—a little guy—every now and then he'd reach over and hit me and jump back and then he'd grin at the other guys as if to say, *Aren't I something?* He was trying to show them that he was quite a man. *This guy you're questioning, I can hit him and jump back.*

I was looking at this little fellow and it was pitiful. I started thinking about these guys—not just negative thoughts about them, but what should be done to them. And I said to myself, *Vivian, what's wrong with you?* These guys are captured by their society; they are of no real consequence. They couldn't help themselves; they couldn't help what they were doing.

It gets back to Jesus's line, "Forgive them, Father, for they know not what they are doing." They have no idea. They're ignorant of what real freedom and justice and truth really is, so how can you sit there and want *them* to get beat up or some other nonsense so they know what it feels like. It's just crazy. So you begin to understand, and you know your job is far more important. You're not there for that kind of nonsense.

I DO NOT MEAN to lionize myself by telling this story. My Freedom Rides experience was hardly unique. Hundreds of brave, committed men and women, young and old, Black and White, participated in the Rides. Many were jailed. Many were beaten.

Postmortems analyzing the impact of the Rides abound. One result cannot be denied. Robert Kennedy, who had reservations about the Rides from the beginning, was finally pressured to act. The images of burning buses, White mobs beating Blacks and Whites, and the participants' collective nonviolent response to these attacks gave him little choice but to order the Interstate Commerce Commission to actually enforce the law of the land. The Commission issued new regulations—effective November 1, 1961— to ensure that Blacks could sit where they wanted on interstate buses and trains and at lunch counters in terminals. Signs reading "White" or "Colored" at bathrooms and drinking fountains also had to come down. Failure to obey these regulations could result in heavy fines.

Another Freedom Rider, Robert Singleton, has offered an interesting postscript to the rides. Singleton, an African American who went on to become a college professor, and his wife Helen were among the few married couples who participated together. As the *Smithsonian* magazine reported back in 2009:

The legacy of the rides "could not have been more poetic," says Robert Singleton, who connects those events to the election of Barack Obama as president. Obama was born in August 1961, just when the riders were languishing in Mississippi jails and prisons, trying to "break the back of segregation for all people, but especially for the children. We put ourselves in harm's way for a child, at the very time he came into this world, who would become our first Black president."

You're Never Too Young to Fight

5

I ended the last chapter with a quotation citing the importance of putting oneself in harm's way for the benefit of a child . . . or an entire generation of children. Two years after the Freedom Rides, the tables were turned. In May 1963, the children of Birmingham, Alabama, put themselves in harm's way for our people's benefit. The action—now known as the Birmingham Children's Crusade—these young African Americans took to fight for the integration of their city was, and remains, a seminal moment in the history of the civil rights movement.

The willingness of these crusaders to risk imprisonment and injury (even death) and the resultant willingness of the powers that be to meet the nonviolent protest of children, *children*, with police dogs and fire hoses demonstrated the depravity of a White establishment desperate to hold onto a most un-Christian, un-American way of life. The iconic images of the Crusade—captured in photographs and on film—shocked a lot of White folk in the North and, equally important, moved politicians in Washington, including President John F. Kennedy. I'm not saying that Birmingham in and of itself bent the arc of justice—it was one of many essential initiatives—but fourteen months after those kids marched, Congress passed the Civil Rights Act of 1964.

In the history of Western civilization, children had never been used as they were in the spring of 1963. Conventional wisdom is that you don't put young people in harm's way, right? So it shouldn't surprise you to learn that the decision to send the children of Birmingham onto what was, in effect, a battlefield was not made lightly or unanimously. I know because I was there. Here is the story to the best of my recollection:

Not too long after the summer of the Freedom Rides, Octavia and I and our five children—Denise, Cordy Jr., Kira, Mark, and Charisse—moved from Nashville to Chattanooga, Tennessee. Octavia was pregnant with our sixth, Albert, at the time. The move was motivated in large part by financial necessity. My employers at the Sunday School Publishing Board for the National Baptist Convention were afraid to let me stay. They thought I was too active in the movement and that my activism might lead to violence directed against them.

As noted, I was also serving as pastor at the First Community Church. That sounds a little more solid than it actually was. The wages were meager, and I really was just filling in for a friend of mine in seminary who was away in the islands. When he announced he was returning, I knew it was time to move on. When the Cosmopolitan Community Church in Chattanooga (say that real fast!) offered me its pulpit, I said yes.

Jim Crow was alive and well when we arrived in the city known as the "Dynamo of Dixie." But in a short time we did much to change the fortunes of Chattanooga's Black people. By "we," I mean a committed group of activists that I was privileged to lead as president of the Chattanooga Voters Council and as a board member of the Tennessee Voters Council. Our effort went beyond registering more African Americans to vote. We wanted to replicate the gains made in Nashville and open up employment opportunities for our community, particularly in Chattanooga's vibrant manufacturing complex. Factories in the city produced familiar products such as Chris-Craft boats and Buster Brown socks. But few African Americans were on the factory floors and none that I can recall were in the corporate offices.

Once again a concerted nonviolent effort in the public square and in the courts achieved great gains. In 1962, the city's public schools were ordered to desegregate by the federal courts. And in 1963, the mayor, Ralph Kelly, ordered all city-owned facilities to open their doors to African Americans. Private commercial establishments like those in Nashville and the factories we pressured also met our demands.

By this time, I had known Dr. King for some years. He knew of my embrace of nonviolent direct action dating back to my days in Peoria and of our success in Nashville. At his request, I'd participated in the Albany Movement in late 1961. This was a not particularly successful effort to increase the number of registered Black voters and fight desegregation in that racially divided Georgia city. The results in Chattanooga were much better.

Martin had also heard me speak. This is one of my favorite stories. At one of the SCLC's national conferences, I'd been ask to fill in for the highly visible U.S. congressman representing Harlem, Adam Clayton Powell Jr. I guess I did pretty well, because when I finished, the organization's co-founder, the Reverend Ralph Abernathy, said, "I move we thank Mr. Powell for not coming."

Shortly after that, Martin asked me to join the leadership of SCLC. Soon I had a new full-time job as SCLC's director of national affiliates. First stop? Birmingham. Martin sent me and SCLC executive director Wyatt Tee Walker there from Atlanta in the early spring of 1963.

BEFORE WE GET TO the debate over whether or not to involve the children in the Birmingham effort, let's take a quick look at the events that precipitated that debate and some of the adults who played critical roles.

SCLC did not initiate the early efforts to integrate what Martin deemed the most segregated city in the United States. In December of 1956, shortly after the Supreme Court's decision in the Montgomery Bus Boycott case, the Reverend Fred Shuttlesworth, pastor of Birmingham's Bethel Baptist Church, announced the formation of the Alabama Christian Movement for Human Rights (ACMHR). For the next six-plus years, he and his organization challenged the segregated "way of life" in the state's most populous city.

This was a dangerous undertaking. Within days of the announcement, persons unknown dynamited Fred's home. Fortunately, he was not only unhurt, but undaunted. When the powers that be suggested that he leave town, he fired back, "I was not born to run." He didn't run in 1957 after he was being beaten and his wife was stabbed. And he didn't run in 1958 after a bomb was found in his church. (I'm proud to say that Fred and I were known as the "Rabble-Rousing Twins"—due to our similar temperaments and the fact that we looked much alike.)

To end discriminatory employment practices and desegregate the city's schools and public facilities as well as restaurants and other stores, ACMHR organized boycotts of Birmingham's businesses. When these failed to effect the desired change, Fred, who was one of the co-founders of SCLC in 1957, asked for our help. And so, under the leadership of Brothers Shuttlesworth and Walker, Project C was born. That's C as in Confrontation. The idea was to focus the country's attention on Birmingham by provoking mass arrests. And what would we do to get arrested in large numbers? Sit-in and march.

Forgive the pun, but when it came to Project C, Wyatt Walker dotted the i's and, of course, crossed the t's. He and local activist Lola Hendricks timed how long marches that began at our headquarters—the 16th Street Baptist Church—would take. He also identified buildings where the marchers could take refuge if attacked.

Martin arrived in Birmingham on April 2. The following day Fred, Lola, and the Reverend Ambus Hill went to the office of City Public Safety Commissioner Eugene "Bull" Connor and requested a permit to march. Connor denied the request and a court quickly issued an injunction prohibiting us from marching without such a permit. It was clear, therefore, that a permit-less march of about fifty people planned for Good Friday, April 12, would result in arrests. It did.

During his one week behind bars, Martin wrote his famous "Letter from Birmingham Jail." Read it, my friends. In this open letter, Martin eloquently states the case for nonviolent direct action and, when necessary, civil disobedience.

The marches and sit-ins continued after Good Friday. But we had a problem. We were running out of protesters. Hundreds were arrested and jailed. But many of the Black citizens of Birmingham simply could not afford to take time away from work to demonstrate, much less go to jail. In addition to the possibility of physical retaliation, the odds were great that they would be fired from their jobs.

What to do? Jim Bevel, who was now SCLC's director of direct action, suggested that the children should march. He and another member of SCLC's inner circle, Dorothy Cotton, were already running workshops in the spirit of Jim Lawson for young people. Because of his conviction to involve children and youth, Martin along with others decided to recruit youngsters from elementary schools, high schools, and colleges. Jim and others taught them what to do in the face of a variety of assaults, including fire hoses and police dogs. He even showed them film of our sit-ins in Nashville.

- May 2, 1963. Hundreds of students—many defying orders from school administrators—gather in Birmingham churches. Orchestrated marches to city hall begin, with small groups embarking at timed intervals. Many of the youngsters are singing hymns. Just as the adults on previous days, these protestors expect to be arrested. And they are. Police wagons and school buses carry some six hundred kids to a jailhouse already housing six hundred adults. The jail is soon filled beyond its capacity of about one thousand. The nation is watching; U.S. Attorney General Bobby Kennedy worries about the use of children, but expresses sympathy for the cause.

- May 3, 1963. "Bull" Connor has a problem. The jail is overflowing, but another one thousand students plan to head downtown. Connor has a plan to avoid further overcrowding the jail. Nip the demonstration in the bud. He announces that those who defy his orders to curtail the march will face water hoses manned by the Birmingham fire department. In one of the great understatements of the civil rights era, the police say *turn back or you'll get wet* to those who ignore Connor's threat—almost everyone. The cops add: *Keep moving forward and you risk attack from German Shepherds who know just what to do to you.*

The marchers do not turn back; they move forward. The firemen draw their weapons—fire hoses—and shoot. The force of the water knocks the nonviolent youngsters to the ground. The water pressure is so strong that some children literally lose the shirts off their backs.

White onlookers snarl at the protesters. Black onlookers throw rocks until Bevel urges restraint. Photographers and network camera crews capture the assault on the children for that evening's news and the next day's newspapers. President Kennedy says the photographs make him "sick." They were "so much more eloquently reported by the news camera than by any number of explanatory words," he adds. Exactly. We all know what a picture is worth. JFK sends Assistant Attorney General Burke Marshall to Birmingham to try and work out a deal between us and the White establishment.

At a huge evening rally, Martin reiterates our commitment to parents and others. "Don't worry about your children who are in jail. The eyes of the world are on Birmingham. We're going on in spite of dogs and fire hoses. We've gone too far to turn back."

- May 6, 1963. The eyes of the nation—indeed, the world—are on Birmingham. The protests continue. Connor creates a temporary jail at the state fairgrounds to house those who can't be accommodated in the filled-to-capacity city jail. Entertainers/activists including Dick Gregory and Joan Baez arrive to demonstrate their support.

The establishment is beginning to crack. White businessmen seem amenable to some sort of compromise. Firefighters refuse Connor's orders to turn their hoses on the next wave of protestors; instead, they actually help clean up the flooded basement of the 16th Street Baptist Church.

- May 7, 1963. More protests. Sit-ins at downtown stores. More fire hoses. One thousand more arrests, bringing the total to about twenty-five hundred. Governor George Wallace deploys state troopers, while the federal government contemplates sending in the National Guard. Estimated number of participants on this day: about three thousand.

- May 8, 1963. Five days after the children first marched, the White business community agrees to most of our demands.

- May 10, 1963. One week after the children first marched, city officials also agree to sweeping reforms ranging from the desegregation of lunch counters and bathrooms to increased hiring of Black men and women. Favorable terms for the release of the young and old still in jail are also set.

- May 11, 1963. It is almost a given that every nonviolent civil rights action provokes a violent reaction. The Black-owned Gaston Motel, Martin's home away from home, is bombed. So, too, is the home of Martin's brother, A. D., who is a minister in Birmingham. Some in our community throw rocks and bottles at the police. As the tensions escalate, some buildings and cars are set aflame. Bobby Kennedy sends in federal troops. Martin preaches nonviolence.

WHILE IT IS TRUE that Birmingham's businesses and government were slow to implement several of the agreed upon reforms, this much is also true: the campaign inspired President Kennedy to accelerate civil rights legislation; work began on what would become the Civil Rights Act of 1964. The campaign also inspired Black activists in other Southern cities to step up desegregation efforts. Sadly, one of these activists, Medgar Evers, was assassinated in the driveway of his Mississippi home on June 12, 1963. Remember the August 28, 1963, March on Washington at which Martin delivered his "I Have a Dream" speech? This, too, had its roots in the Birmingham crusade.

I should also note that Birmingham vaulted Martin and SCLC into even greater national and international prominence and respect. After being named *Time* magazine's "Man of the Year" in 1963, Martin was awarded the 1964 Nobel Peace Prize. In 2011, Taylor Branch and I discussed the Birmingham Campaign almost fifty years after its occurrence. Here is an excerpt of that discussion:

BRANCH: All right. The decision. Because even after Dr. King came out of jail in Birmingham, before those big dogs and hoses marches, the Birmingham movement was almost on life support and Bevel and Dorothy Cotton and the people running those youth workshops said, *We're not out of volunteers yet, we've got these young people.* And lots of people have talked about debates within the movement over whether to use young people and how young to use them.

VIVIAN: That was a real argument—what should happen. Bevel was the one that really said young people should go, right? That you're never too young to fight for your freedom became the thing for all of us, but I mean it was Bevel who brought it up and really fought for it, and Diane (Nash), of course. They were married at the time.

But that changed things. It's the only place—I want to say in the Western world, but it's the only place in nonviolent work I know in the West where there was a children's movement. Do you know the other part of it where they get out to jail, because when the people that Sunday (May 5), when people come out and go out to the jail to sing to their kids and the firemen refused to turn the hoses on them?

BRANCH: That's a great story. . . . But the decision to use children—and you're absolutely right. I wrote in one of my prefaces that the only parallel that I know of is the Passover story, where the children in Egypt had—

VIVIAN: Talk about going back.

BRANCH: But I mean, where people that young have that kind of historical impact.

VIVIAN: That's exactly right. It just didn't happen. In fact, this is why there was an argument against using them, because it was thought—everybody thought, oh, you shouldn't use children. Why not, right? But I think one of the reasons is because most adults weren't ready to do it, period—much less have children do it.

Listen, I remember doing that thing, having kids out of one of the high schools—high schools are like small colleges, right? And they were coming out of windows, coming down, and you reminded me when you said that one of my arguments I was making to the kids is that it had been raining one morning when I went over there, and the stream was coming through the schoolyard, and I told them, "Cross over Jordan, baby. Let's go. Let's go do it." And we did, and we did, and they were right with it.

Listen, they so badly wanted to come out, the principal had to so badly keep them in. They locked the doors, and so the kids were crawling out of windows and jumping down from that second floor because the first floor's always a little higher. They were coming down and hanging down and falling and jumping out of windows so that they could go on out and do it. There was no doubt in the kids' minds, none at all.

BRANCH: No, but plenty in the adults' minds.

VIVIAN: That's exactly right, but not in the kids' minds. I think that the adults were afraid they may be blamed for something, you see what I mean? Rather than—because all of us in Birmingham knew, everybody in Birmingham was part of the movement. But then like so many things, you never knew what the police were going to do to them.

BRANCH: For all the argument and the resistance of the parents in Birmingham, there were arguments in practically every Black home in Birmingham about what to do with this. Should we let our children do it? Should we keep them from doing it? It's also true, though, that a lot of the parents who didn't want their children involved—practically none did—were converted by their children when they actually did it. There's this famous story of the woman walking along the line, all upset that she sees her eight-year-old marching, and then she says, "Sing, children, sing," because . . .

VIVIAN: She changed her mind.

BRANCH: She just kind of gave into it, so that happened.

VIVIAN: "Sing, children, sing." I never heard that one, but I love it, because whether it's true or not, it gets the whole feeling of everything that happened, the stuff that happened. But I was very clear that everybody wanted it to happen. Now, not that—when I say, *everybody*, it's over two hundred. There was a lot of argument, but I don't think it was nearly as intense as it seems, because—and when the children went to jail, that did change everything. There was no longer anything but I think it was no longer because they knew they wouldn't be hurt, right?

BRANCH: Mm-hmm.

VIVIAN: But the story to me is more so than the kids going is their parents coming out.

WYATT TEE WALKER DESCRIBED the 1963 initiative in Birmingham and the 1965 effort in Selma as "Siamese twins" joining to "kill segregation . . . and bury the body." I'll get to Selma in the next chapter. But before doing so, let's revisit another critical but decidedly lesser-known campaign related to those twins. St. Augustine, Florida, 1964.

Martin used to say, "It's a ten-day world." He meant that after ten days, people forget events, even important events. We knew that as big as Birmingham and the March on Washington were, we needed to keep the momentum going. America had started to look at itself in the mirror. We were beginning to win over a portion of the public by demonstrating our commitment to nonviolence. The White House and Congress were drafting a civil rights act. And federal judges like the Honorable Frank M. Johnson Jr. (Middle District of Alabama—he presided over so many civil rights cases) were being asked to make decisions crucial to the integration of the South.

Settled in 1564, St. Augustine lays claim to being the USA's oldest city. As it prepared to celebrate its four hundredth birthday in 1964, it was also one of the country's most racially divided cities—a prime target for our next desegregation effort. At least that was my thinking when Martin sent me there to survey the situation. With the anniversary and the tourists coming through there and all of the meaning of that, this was the time to be there.

One of the first things I did when I got down there was start a teaching center down by the market where the slave auctions had taken place. The market had become a tourist attraction, a place where some came to have lunch. My aim was to educate passersby as well as those who came specifically for the workshops. I hoped they would listen to us as they ate, hear our message, understand where we were coming from.

The complete story of that effort could fill a book. In fact, it has. I direct you to *Racial Change and Community Crisis: St. Augustine, Florida, 1877–1980*, by David R. Colburn. The book was a primary source for the following overview offered by the Martin Luther King, Jr. Research and Education Institute at Stanford University:

- July 1963. After learning of federal funding for the celebration of St. Augustine's four hundredth anniversary celebration in 1964, Martin writes a letter of protest to the White House. Why should one of the nation's most segregated cities receive taxpayer dollars for events sure to exclude its Black population?

The racial inequities and tension become increasingly apparent over the coming weeks. Klansmen and other White thugs attack a local group protesting segregated businesses. The group's leader, local dentist/NAACP advisor Robert B. Hayling, is badly beaten, as are three other protesters. Sadly, as was so typical of the day, Hayling and the other victims are convicted of assaulting their attackers.

- December 1963. Local activists ask for SCLC support after the NAACP calls for Hayling's resignation.

- Early spring 1964. I visit St. Augustine, then report back to the SCLC board that we should provide the requested support. Why? There's too much white supremacist activity and too little leadership from the local clergy and others. They could use our help.

Within weeks, as Stanford's King Institute notes, "Martin Luther King Jr. and the SCLC launched a massive campaign supporting the small local movement to end racial discrimination in the nation's oldest city. King hoped that demonstrations there would lead to local desegregation and that media attention would garner national support for the Civil Rights Act of 1964, which was then stalled in a congressional filibuster."

- Late March 1964. Our effort included enlisting sympathetic White college students—mostly from the North—to join marches and sit-ins during Easter week. The result? "Hundreds were jailed. Some were made to stand in a cramped outdoor overflow pen in the summer heat, while others were put into a concrete 'sweatbox' overnight. Bail rose from $100 per person up to $1,000," write the Stanford folk.

- May 1964. Martin comes down from Atlanta on May 18. Ten days later Martin tells those assembled at a local Baptist church that an end to the city's segregation is imminent "because trouble don't last always." But two days later the house he's staying in is shot up in an early morning drive-by. No one is hurt, fortunately.

These headlines from articles published in the *New York Times* between June 1, 1964, and July 15, 1964, provide an instructive timeline of what was happening on the ground . . . and in the water. You get the sense of the ebb and flow of an effort to overturn centuries of injustice.

Five Are Arrested in Sit-in at St. Augustine Motel

Police-Klan Ties Hinted in Florida

Dr. King Describes St. Augustine As Most Lawless City He's Seen; Reports Threats on His Life in Florida—Shots Are Fired Into a Negro's Automobile

Klan Is an Issue in St. Augustine; Negroes Link It to Violence —Whites Discount Role

Dr. King's Beach Cottage Is Ransacked by Vandals

Marchers Beaten in St. Augustine; Integrationists Rally after Judge Nullifies City Ban

Police Rout Mob at St. Augustine; Tear Gas and Dogs Disperse Whites Attacking Negroes

Martin Luther King and 17 Others Jailed Trying to Integrate St. Augustine Restaurant

200 Whites March at St. Augustine; They Stage an Anti-Rights Parade in Negro Area

South Girds for Crisis; Massive Assault on Racial Barriers Planned for This Summer Creates Atmosphere of Tension

37 More Jailed in St. Augustine; Negroes Arrested at Church and Restaurant Sit-ins

50 More Demonstrators Jailed in St. Augustine

White Beach Integrated

Dr. King's Plea Moves 17 Rabbis to Join in St. Augustine Protest

16 Rabbis Arrested as Pool Dive-In Sets off St. Augustine Rights Clash

Whites Repulsed in St. Augustine; Police Block Their Attempt to Get at Negro Marchers

Marches Curbed at St. Augustine; Governor Bars Night Moves as Melee Erupts at Beach

Two Races March in St. Augustine; Negroes Will Appeal Ban on Night Processions

Racists Break Up Florida Wade-Ins

New Racial Clash Halted in Florida; Police Guard Integrationists at Beach and on March

Dr. King Requests U.S. And in Florida; Asks White House to Send Mediator to St. Augustine

St. Augustine Mob Attacks Negroes; 19 Hospitalized as Whites Run Wild—Police Seize, Then Free, 5 Assailants

St. Augustine Aides Say They Cannot Keep Peace

St. Augustine's Leaders Moving For a Biracial Peace Committee

Police Hold Off Florida Racists; Guard a Rights Wade-in and Parade in St. Augustine

Peace Unit Named for St. Augustine; Dr. King Calls Off Protests After a Four-Man Panel Is Named by Governor

Civil Rights Bill to Be Law Tonight; President to Sign Measure in a Televised Ceremony

Critical Test for the Nonviolent Way; In St. Augustine, Martin Luther King Has Put His Doctrine of Nonviolence on Trial: By Making It Succeed There, He Hopes to Win Over Those Negroes Now Veering Toward Extremism.

4 Negroes Beaten at St. Augustine

I can add a little more information about the beaches and the marches. You've probably heard someone describe an unpleasant experience as "no day at the beach." Well, we had a few of those, literally, in St. Augustine.

Shortly after World War II, the Negro Professional and Businessman's League expressed the goal of achieving safe access to public beaches and pools in Broward County, Florida—much of which, including Fort Lauderdale, sits on the Atlantic Ocean. Black activists in other cities and counties launched similar initiatives because throughout the state there were separate beaches and pools for Blacks and Whites. Separate and *unequal* in terms of location, amenities, and everything else you can imagine.

St. Augustine, 1964, was no different. So in addition to desegregating businesses, we were determined to gain access to the city's public (in other words, Whites-only) beaches. The Global Nonviolent Action Database offers a comprehensive report on Florida "wade-ins" between 1945 and 1964. Here's what it says about ours.

On 17 June, 1964, the campaign had reached St. Augustine. A successful two-hour-long wade-in by thirty-five people drew attention and garnered some Black and White support. On June 24th, however, White beachgoers did not allow waders to reach the water by physically blockading the shore. Due to the court-ordered desegregation, the police had no choice but to protect the Black activists from the threat of violence by the White crowd, but they did not aid them in reaching their objective. That night, White groups, such as the National States Rights Party, conducted anti-Black speeches, and three hundred Whites marched to protest integrating the beaches.

The next day, African Americans in St. Augustine famously planned to "beat the heat and segregation" by entering Monson Motor Lodge, an "integration testing ground" for Dr. Martin Luther King Jr. and the SCLC. As Black swimmers enjoyed the pool, the hotel manager poured a bottle of acid into the water and an off-duty policeman eventually jumped into the pool to beat the non-cooperative swimmers. The swimmers were arrested, but photos of the injustice began to circulate around the world, infuriating many as a symbol of "barbaric racism." The local Grand Jury asked Dr. King to leave St. Augustine.

On 22 June, police arrested twenty-two waders. State Senator Verle Pope offered himself as a mediator to a biracial committee to address the tensions. He was deemed by some an ally to the African American community, and local Whites smashed the windows in his office. A Danish photographer who recorded the wade-ins was also brutally beaten.

In the most violent incident, on 25 June, Whites, including police, attacked seventy-five people during a wade-in. Later that night, five hundred White people attacked demonstrators in St. Augustine, including SCLC leader C. T. Vivian, and hospitalized nineteen people, many of whom were in severe condition.

I described my experience at one of the wade-ins to Taylor Branch:

We couldn't swim on the beach, right? Here are sixteen hundred feet of beach and you couldn't swim on it because if you went in they would drown you. . . . All the White guys were on the beach and they swam all the time, so what they would do is to create like a net, like a human net.

I was leading [a wade-in]. Fred Shuttlesworth came out from nowhere and joined me. Fred said, "Can you swim?"

I said, "Yeah, but not in an ocean . . ."

A guy jumped on top of me and took me right to the bottom. He's on top of me. Well, as I said, I can't swim in an ocean. I used to teach at the YMCA in a pool, but I didn't do it in the ocean, and my face was in the sand and I said—and I laughed to myself, "This is it." I knew I wasn't going to get out from underneath this guy, and my face was already in the sand. And right after that there was a jerk. Phew! I shot straight to the top. A policeman had come over and jerked this guy off of me. I didn't see any police . . . but the guy who was a policeman, he pulled the guy off of me, I shot to the surface, and then he started to arrest me. And I said, "You don't arrest me. He's the guy that jumped on me. I got a right to be on this ocean."

And he looked back and forth and this guy ran because he knew I was right. This guy ran and the policeman was caught between, and he was afraid to go get him because he was still thinking about what I said, and then he decided that I was right, so he was very nice from that time on. He took me out to the beach and got me towels and everything. He was very nice then.

As I also told Taylor, we marched by land as well as by sea.

The midnight bell [from the Episcopal church next to the old slave market], would go on the church tower, and—*boom, boom*—as it would go off, we would march, and there could be all these guys waiting to do you in because they were trying to stop you from marching.

Hosea [Williams] created the midnight march, but one night Dorothy Cotton and I were leading the group. We were coming in not right there in the front [of the market]. It was around the side somehow, and the policeman would not let us into the slave market area. They cut us off and wouldn't let us into it.

Well, they knew something we did not know. The Klan or Hoss Manucy's guys were there waiting for us, and they had chains and steel bars and all kinds of stuff. So we stopped there and prayed, but we couldn't move on. That was the night that Dorothy talks about when we were praying and she said something or somebody prayed to God, and this guy says, "Niggers ain't got no god." [Hoss Manucy was the leader of a Klan-like group of white supremacists, a virulent racist who was on the list of the local sheriff's special deputies.]

I was leading another midnight march when about forty of us were sent to the hospital. You have that old Mexican kind of wall around things, and [the Klan or Manucy's guys] would throw stuff over the walls onto us as we marched down the sidewalk, and we'd have to move over to the middle of the street. Those walls are so beautiful in the daytime, but at night they were dangerous, man. They would climb up on the walls and throw stuff down on us, right? I remember that night was when we went back to a church to regroup but I knew I couldn't stop [the marching] because here again, we won't let violence stop nonviolence. And so once it gave people time to get themselves together, and I gave another speech and there was another guy with me from the movement, and I gave him a speech.

Then I said, "Whether anybody goes or not, I'm going," and I stepped off this little platform and started down the aisle, and I didn't know whether they were coming or not.

It's one of those nights you don't really know, but you know the only way you're going to find out is you've got to go, and so I started walking down the aisle. I got about halfway there, and I saw them look behind me and they were coming out the aisles and joining in to walk on out. And I remember a woman sort of getting up, unclear whether she really wanted to go, but she had made up her mind she was going, and she walked to the center aisle and came on out, too, and down the street we went.

We went down the street at my next major stop, as well. Selma, 1965. Before we go there, a postscript. The landmark Civil Rights Act was passed on July 1, 1964. It changed our lives. But it did not end the dangers we continued—continue to this day—to face. As Stanford's King Institute, referencing Colburn, observed:

Despite this national success, Black residents in St. Augustine continued to face violence and intimidation. Consistent threats and picketing by the Klan led many of the town's businesses to remain segregated. Although SCLC continued to provide some financial support to activists in St. Augustine beyond July 1964, the organization never returned to the city. King observed that St. Augustine had been made to "bear the cross," suffering violence and brutality that helped prompt Congress to pass the Civil Rights Act of 1964.

6

We're Willing to Be Beaten

On March 25, 1965, Martin spoke to some twenty-five thousand folks of all colors, ages, and religious persuasion gathered at the steps of the Alabama state capitol. Many in the crowd had spent the last five days marching fifty-four miles from Selma to Montgomery. Others had joined the march along the way. Thousands more had fallen in as the trek drew to a conclusion.

Over his too-short lifetime, Martin gave numerous memorable speeches. His remarks—known now as the "How Long, Too Long" speech—on this historic occasion are rightfully considered among his finest. Let me begin this chapter with one line that is particularly relevant to the story that follows: "The confrontation of good and evil compressed in the tiny community of Selma generated the massive power to turn the whole nation to a new course."

Amen. No doubt many of you know a fair amount about the voting rights effort centered in Selma and nearby Marion, Alabama, that put the nation on that new course after SCLC arrived in January 1965. In all likelihood you're aware of Bloody Sunday, the first attempt to march from Selma to Montgomery in memory of Jimmie Lee Jackson, a twenty-six-year-old church deacon and pulpwood cutter. Jimmie Lee was shot in Marion by James Bonard Fowler, a White Alabama state trooper, after Governor George Wallace's minions attacked peaceful protestors on February 18, 1965. He died in the hospital eight days later.

That initial attempt on March 7, 1965—led by John Lewis and Hosea Williams—was thwarted by a horrific assault by tear gas-throwing and billy club-wielding troopers and vigilantes on six hundred peaceful marchers on the Edmund Pettus Bridge. Dozens were injured. Sixteen were hospitalized.

I was not on that march, nor was Martin. Indeed, with the exception of Hosea, few members of the SCLC braintrust were present. As was our practice, one or two of us stayed in Selma for the weekend and the rest returned home to Atlanta—to see families, sleep in one's own bed, recharge.

I only learned about Bloody Sunday that night when the news hit the television airwaves. ABC actually interrupted the movie it was show-ing—*Judgment at Nuremberg*, ironically—to show the sickening images. Remember there was no cable TV in those days, only the three networks, and some forty-eight million people were watching the star-studded Academy Award-winning film. Many of those viewers were in the North, of course, and the impact those images from Selma had on them can't be overstated. We won a lot of support that night thanks to Governor Wallace and his stooges.

Truth be told, an undertaking of this magnitude should have waited until we were all there. But there wasn't unanimity within our ranks for the march. Hosea was the most enthusiastic, and he was able to point to the fact that John was equally enthusiastic, as were many local Black citizens, including Selma's highly respected activist Mrs. Amelia Boynton.

You may also know about a second march two days after Bloody Sunday. This one is known as Turnaround Tuesday because Martin and local citizens and hundreds of sympathetic clergy and White folk from around the country willingly reversed course after reaching the bridge and praying. One of those White clergy, the Reverend James Reeb, was beaten by racist thugs hours afterwards and died two days later.

These two marches and that successful effort later in the month on attempt number three led directly to what many consider the most im-portant piece of legislation in the latter half of the twentieth century, the Voting Rights Act of 1965.

It's not my purpose here to tell the complete story of the Selma cam-paign and the history of the fight for our voting rights. Many fine books are devoted to this subject, including my brother John Lewis's trilogy, *March*, and Taylor Branch's *Pillar of Fire* and *At Canaan's Edge*. Rather, what I want to do here is give you a brief overview of the campaign and then focus on a few memorable moments from those days: primarily the

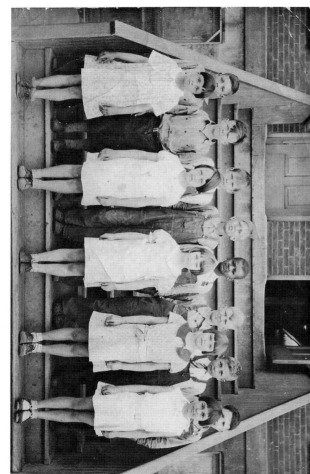

Top left and middle: C.T. Vivian sitting in chair, circa 1928, and in his Sunday best with playmate.

Top right: Grandmother Anna Woods Tindell sitting on running board with C.T. Vivian, circa 1930.

Above: Third-grade class, 1933.

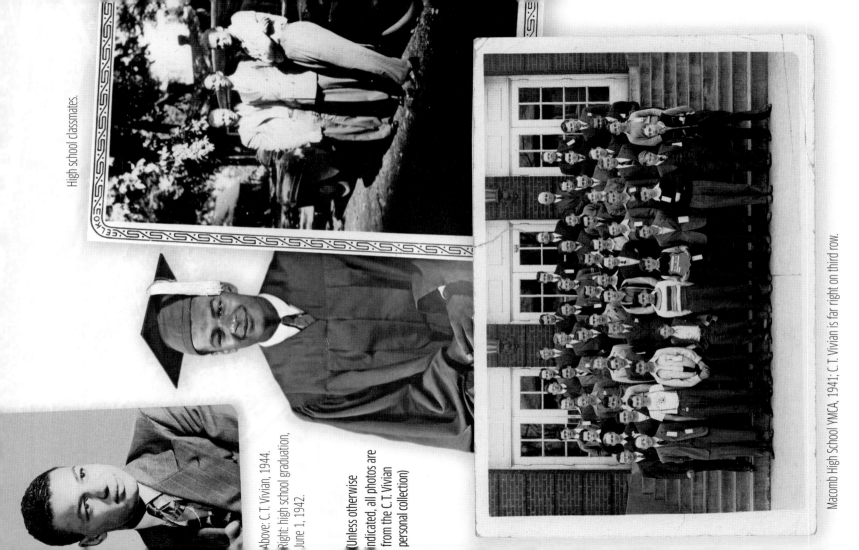

High school classmates.

Above: C. T. Vivian, 1944.

Right: high school graduation, June 1, 1942.

(Unless otherwise indicated, all photos are from the C. T. Vivian personal collection)

Macomb High School YMCA, 1941; C. T. Vivian is far right on third row.

C. T. Vivian's maternal family – *Back row:* grandmother, Annie Woods Tindell; grandfather, James A. Tindell; great-uncles, Lewis E. Woods and Anderson Brooks Woods; great-aunt, Russella Woods Wilhite. *Front row:* mother, Euzetta Tindell (Vivian) Huff; great-grandmother, Handy Sampson Woods; great-great-grandparents, Al and Clarinda Sampson; uncle, Albert Brooks Tindell; great-grandfather, David E. Woods. (Handy, Al, Clarinda, and David were all born prior to Emancipation.)

No image is available of Robert Vivian, C. T. Vivian's father.

Back: first wife (1945-1948), Jane Amanda Lee Teague; daughter, Jo Anna Vivian; C. T. Vivian. Front: mother, Euzetta Tindell (Vivian) Huff; great-grandfather, David E. Woods; grandmother, Anna Woods Tindell Mayo; Anna's 2nd husband, George Washington Mayo.

Hattie & Uncle Albert

Above: Aunt Hattie and Uncle Albert Tindell, circa 1937.
Middle: C.T. Vivian in his teen years.
Right: Euzetta Tindell Huff and her second husband, Mr. Huff, circa 1950.

Five generations, circa 1947 – C.T. Vivian, daughter Jo Anna Vivian, mother Euzetta Tindell Huff, great-grandfather David E. Woods, and grandmother Anna Woods Tindell Mayo.

C. T. Vivian meets the love of his life

C. T. Vivian and Willie Octavia Gean marry on February 23, 1953, in Peoria, Illinois.

Below: Willie Octavia Gean high school picture, 1946.

Bottom right: Octavia & C. T. Vivian in their archival library, the largest personal book collection in the Southeast.

C. T. Vivian joins the Nashville movement

Left: C. T. Vivian and Diane Nash lead a march through downtown Nashville, Tennessee *(Courtesy Nashville Public Library, Special Collection, Jack Corn / The Tennessean)*

Right: James Lawson, essential in student training in nonviolence theology.

Above: Mississippi National Guardsman standing on a bus next to freedom riders C. T. Vivian and Jim Bevel.

Right: C. T. Vivian stepping into a Jackson, Mississippi, police wagon after his 1961 arrest. *(Both photos by Paul Schutzer/The LIFE Picture Collection ©Meredith Corporation)*

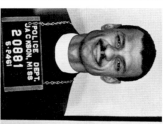

C. T. Vivian mug shot, May 24, 1961.

C. T. Vivian pushes hard in Selma

C. T. Vivian praying on the Dallas County courthouse steps before helmeted Sheriff Jim Clark stopped him at the door with a court order, Selma, Alabama, February 5, 1965. (© *Horace Court /AP*)

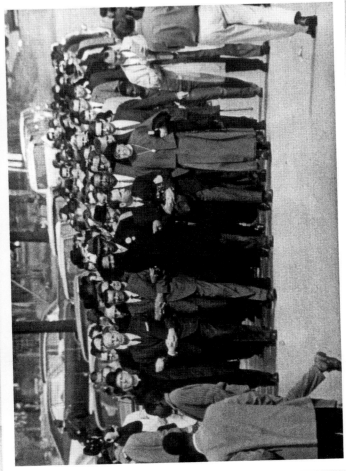

C. T. Vivian, civil rights leaders, and clergy leading demonstrators and mourners to the Reverend James Reeb's funeral in Selma, Alabama, March 15, 1965. (*UPI*)

Left: C.T. Vivian, right, and John Lewis, left, flank the casket of Martin Luther King Jr. on the Morehouse College campus, April 9, 1968.

C. T. Vivian emerges on the national stage

This page, background: top, C. T. Vivian giving comfort to "Daddy King" at Martin Luther King Jr.'s funeral service, April 1968; below right, a hand-written note by Martin Luther King Jr. *(King Papers Collection)*

Facing page, top: C. T. Vivian walking toward the pulpit while the audience claps, including Martin Luther King Jr, Ralph Abernathy, and Rosa Parks in the chancel, Birmingham, Alabama, 1963. *(Collection of the Smithsonian National Museum of African American History and Culture, Gift of Monica Karales and the Estate of James Karales)*

Facing page, bottom: SCLC strategy session, from left, Hosea Williams, Martin Luther King Jr, Ralph Abernathy, James Bevel on floor in center, and C. T. Vivian.

Below: C. T. Vivian and Martin Luther King Jr. discuss SCLC business.

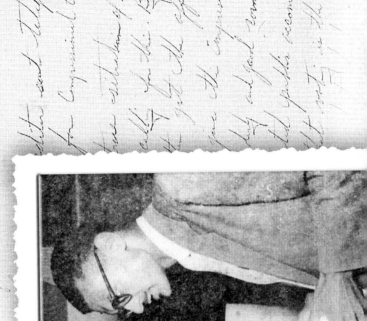

C. T. Vivian confronting police in labor protest, Chicago, 1966.

C. T. Vivian with Chicago gang leaders as they gather to protest.

C. T. Vivian teaching nonviolent methods to Chicago gang leaders.

C.T. Vivian leads press conference, with Joseph E. Lowery to his right.

Name: VIVIAN, C. T., N/M
DOB 7/30/24, 4'10", 150 lbs.,
brown eyes, black hair.
Address: Chattanooga, Tennessee
Occ.: Director of Affiliates
S C L C
Arrest: 5/24/61 Breach of Peace
Organization: Member of S C L C
and is a Freedom Rider.
Associates: Martin Luther King,
Jr., Ralph D. Abernathy, Fred
Lee Shuttlesworth and Andrew Young.
Note: A subversive background.

C.T. Vivian's photo and description in Alabama's "Individuals Active in Civil Disturbances" file. Like those of many other civil rights activists, his card notes "a subversive background."

C.T. Vivian, third from right, in solidarity with others during an SCLC demonstration.

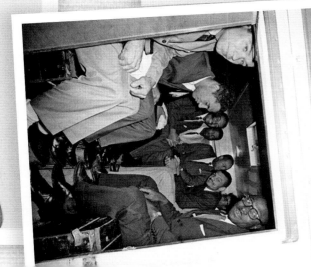

Below: C.T. Vivian with other Freedom Riders, including John Lewis and James Farmer, being moved to the Hinds County Prison Farm in Jackson. He was released May 29, 1961 after the press reported he had been beaten by guards. *(AP Images)*

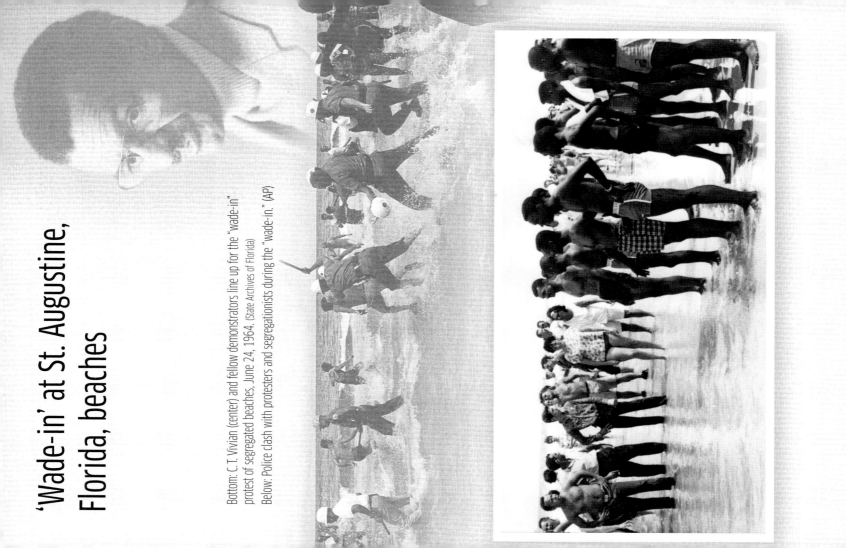

'Wade-in' at St. Augustine, Florida, beaches

Bottom: C. T. Vivian (center) and fellow demonstrators line up for the "wade-in" protest of segregated beaches, June 24, 1964. (State Archives of Florida)

Below: Police clash with protesters and segregationists during the "wade-in." (AP)

Left: with Fidel Castro.
Center left: preaching.
Center right: marching for justice.
Bottom: "Bloody Sunday" commemorative march in Selma,
Alabama; to C. T. Vivian's left are Martin Luther King III,
Coretta Scott King, and Amelia Boynton Robinson.

Left: Cartoon in *Chicago Daily Defender*, November 11, 1969.

Center left: C.T. Vivian accepts Walk of Fame honor in Atlanta, Georgia, 2009; behind him is Father Michael Pfleger. *(Photo Bob Morgan)*

Below: with long-time friend, civil rights supporter, and comedian Dick Gregory.

Below left: with long-time friend and fellow activist Father Jim Morton.

Below right: C.T. Vivian witnessing as Yasser Arafat signs a document in Lebanon.

C.T. Vivian given highest civilian honor

Above left, Chatting with Jimmy Carter at the America's Sunday Supper, August 11, 2013. *(Photo by Maria Saporta)*

Above right: with Stacey Abrams and Oprah Winfrey.

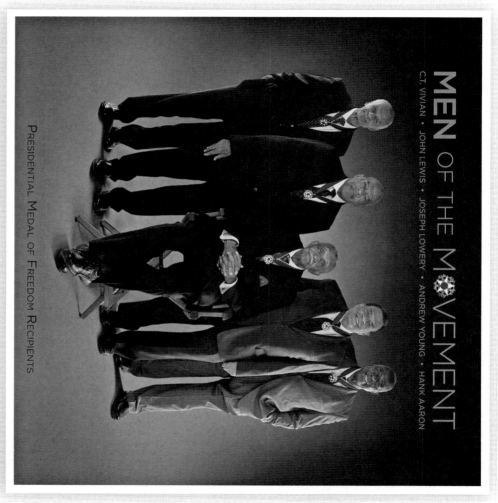

C.T. Vivian, John Lewis, Joseph E. Lowery, Andrew Young, and Henry "Hank" Aaron receive Presidential Medal of Honor, November 26, 2013. *(© Photo J.D. Scott in conjunction with Studio Named Bermudez, Atlanta, Georgia)*

MEN OF THE MOVEMENT

C.T. VIVIAN • JOHN LEWIS • JOSEPH LOWERY • ANDREW YOUNG • HANK AARON

PRESIDENTIAL MEDAL OF FREEDOM RECIPIENTS

C.T. Vivian, center right, meets with President Obama and committee to discuss incarceration reform, September 24, 2016. *(White House Photo)*

With Juanita Abernathy, Andrew Young, Coretta Scott King, and Joseph E. Lowery at the Morehouse Leadership Conference.

The Vivian Family

Children

Jo Anna Vivian Walker
Denise Vivian Morse (Carlton)
Cordy Tindell Vivian Jr. *(deceased)*
Kira E. Vivian
Mark E. Vivian (Utrophia)
Anita Charisse Thornton (Andre)
Al Vivian (DeAna Jo)

Grandchildren

Kirsten Yvette Vivian
Katrina Dionne Garner
Kerry Jemal Walker Sr. *(deceased)*
Kyra DeVette Walker
Kafi Tamu Walker *(deceased)*
Marlene Vivian Whitsett Vaughn (John)
Larri Denise Whitsett Rose (Michael)

Mark E. Vivian II
Albert Louis Vivian II
Coleman Vivian
Andre Thornton, II
Demetrius Taggart
Micah Vivian
Kendall Taggart

Great Grandchildren

Kai Ayana Walker *(deceased)*
Kamara Antoine Davis
Kori Nicole Davis
Kamron LaMar Causey *(deceased)*
Kerry Jemal Walker Jr. (Corrine)
Kerrington DeMere Walker
Keenen Jerome Walker (Ayeasha)
Katrina DeVette Walker
Kedeem Langston Walker
Kiera Jo Ann Walker
Kenadee Tamu Walker
JuWan Wata Garner
Asia Smith
Sanaa Amara Rose
Cairo Timothy (C.T.) Rose
Ava Ivy Ann Vaughn

Great Great Grandchildren

Kamara Harris
A'Kyla Davis
Keenan Harris
Myair Lee
Zalandous Bassett
Courion Walker
Kamerion Causey
Kaliyah Walker
Karrington Walker Jr.
C'Ante' Cagle
Kaiyana Friend
Kamiya Causey
Kelly Walker
Kalease Causey
Nyell Sanders
Keyion Walker
Camryn Bragg
Cordero Ivory
King Franklin
Sanaai Davis
Karter Johnson
Khalil Walker
Austin Russell
Kenya Walker
Kamani Davis
Kamarii Walker
Kylan Lee
Kerryion Walker

Great Great Great Grandchildren

Kash Adams
K'Lani Harris

Great Grandchildren

Cameron Taggart
Jeremiah Taggart
Jasmine Taggart
Trinity Taggart
Hannah Taggart
Kealen Taggart
Toraz Miller
Kirsten Elizabeth Aaron

C. T. Vivian, staff person, and Bawa Jain, Olso, Norway.

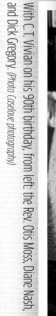

With C.T. Vivian on his 90th birthday, from left: the Rev. Otis Moss, Diane Nash, and Dick Gregory. *(Photo Caselove photography)*

The Reverends James Lawson and C.T. Vivian explaining nonviolence; the former trained the latter.

C. T. Vivian among a group with the 14th Dalai Lama.

Nonviolent activists Bernard Lafayette and C.T. Vivian.

With Donald Bermudez and Congressman John Lewis at Presidential Freedom photo shoot, November 26, 2013.

Don Rivers with C.T. Vivian at his 90th Birthday Celebration July 2015, Atlanta.

Enjoying a laugh with, from left, the Reverend Joseph E Lowery, Father Michael Pfleger, and Minister Louis Farrakhan.

At the Morehouse College Candle in the Dark Gala, 2001, from left: Horace T. Ward, Ray Charles, Ezra C. Davidson Jr., Charles "Chuck" H. James III, President Walter E. Massey, Harry Belafonte, Howard F. Jeter, C.T. Vivian, and Dick Gregory.

The Reverend Gerald Durley and C.T Vivian.

The 35th Anniversary of "Bloody Sunday," on the Edmund Pettus Bridge in Selma, Alabama.

confrontation between Sheriff Jim Clark and me on the steps of the Dallas County Courthouse in Selma.

The following timeline, which I've lightly edited, was compiled by Rick Harmon of the *Montgomery Advertiser* and published in *USA Today* in March 2015 on the occasion of the fiftieth anniversary of Bloody Sunday. It doesn't include every event, but it gives you a good sense of how we continued the fight for civil rights and in particular voting rights after Birmingham and St. Augustine.

- 1962–1963—Representatives of the Student Nonviolent Coordinating Committee come to Selma and begin staging protests.

- October 7, 1963—In what would be known as "Freedom Day," about 350 blacks line up to register to vote at the Dallas County Courthouse. Registrars go as slowly as possible and take a two-hour lunch break. Few manage to register, but the protest is considered a huge victory by civil rights advocates.

- July 9, 1964—Circuit Court Judge James Hare issues an injunction effectively forbidding gatherings of three or more people to discuss civil rights or voter registration in Selma.

- December 28, 1964—Dr. King presents the SCLC plan, the "Project for an Alabama Political Freedom Movement," a plan conceived by Jim Bevel that calls for mass action and voter registration attempts in Selma and Dallas County.

- January 2, 1965—King begins his Selma campaign when about seven hundred African Americans show up for a meeting at Brown Chapel in defiance of the injunction.

- January 18, 1965—Black civil rights advocates meet at Brown Chapel. Following speeches and prayers, King and John Lewis lead three hundred marchers out of the church. Selma Director of Public Safety Wilson Baker allows them to march in small groups to the courthouse to register despite Hare's injunction, but Sheriff Jim Clark has them line up in an alley beside the courthouse, where they are out of sight, and leaves them there. None is registered.

- January 22, 1965—Since local teachers can be fired, few have taken overt roles in the civil rights movement, but Margaret Moore and the

Reverend F.D. Reese, who is also a teacher at Hudson High, organize the unprecedented teachers' march. Almost every Black teacher in Selma—110 of them—marches to register to vote. Clark and his deputies push them down the courthouse stairs three times, but they are not arrested.

- February 1, 1965—King and Ralph Abernathy lead a protest and refuse to break into smaller groups. Both are arrested and placed in the Selma jail and refuse to be bonded out.

- February 4, 1965—One day after addressing students at Tuskegee Institute, Malcolm X speaks to a crowd at Brown Chapel, carefully avoiding speaking about his previous differences with King concerning nonviolence.

- February 6, 1965—President Johnson says he will urge Congress to enact a voting rights bill during the session.

- February 18, 1965—Trooper James Bonard Fowler shoots Jimmie Lee Jackson, who dies eight days later.

- February 19, 1965—Governor George Wallace bans nighttime demonstrations in Selma and Marion, and assigns seventy-five troopers to enforce the ban.

- March 5, 1965—King flies to Washington to speak with President Johnson about the Voting Rights Bill. Then he announces the plan for a massive march from Selma to Montgomery.

- March 6, 1965—Alabama Whites, calling themselves the Concerned White Citizens of Alabama, come to Selma to march in support of Black rights. Klan members have followed them into town to protest their march, and the demonstration breaks up as it is clear violence is about to break out.

- March 7, 1965—"Bloody Sunday." National coverage of the event galvanizes the country, and King calls for volunteers from throughout the nation to come to Selma for another march on March 9.

- March 8, 1965—Fred Gray and the SCLC file *Hosea Williams v. George Wallace* before U.S. District Judge Frank M. Johnson Jr. in Montgomery, asking the court to prevent state troopers from blocking the march. . . . Johnson, concerned about the safety of the marchers, says the march should be put off until the court can hold a formal hearing and make a decision.

- March 9, 1965—Turnaround Tuesday. After a brief march, James Reeb, a Unitarian Universalist minister who had come from Boston, is beaten severely by segregationists on a Selma street. He dies of head injuries two days later at the age of thirty-eight.

- March 15, 1965—President Johnson addresses Congress in support of a Voting Rights Bill, quoting the famous civil rights cry "We shall overcome."

- March 17, 1965—Judge Johnson rules in favor of the marchers after receiving a U.S. Justice Department plan outlining their protection during the march. Wallace blasts Johnson's ruling, saying the state cannot afford to provide the security the marchers need and that he will ask the federal government for help.

- March 20, 1965—President Johnson issues an executive order authorizing the federal use of the Alabama National Guard to supply protection. He also sends one thousand military policemen and two thousand Army troops to escort the march from Selma.

- March 21, 1965—About eight thousand people assemble at Brown Chapel before starting the five-day march to Montgomery's Capitol.

- March 24, 1965—Marchers rest . . . on the outskirts of Montgomery, where Harry Belafonte, Tony Bennett, Joan Baez, Sammy Davis Jr., Nina Simone, Frankie Laine and Peter, Paul and Mary perform at a "Stars for Freedom" rally.

- March 25, 1965—The marchers reach Montgomery for a final rally at the Capitol. King speaks. That night, Viola Liuzzo, a White mother of five who had driven from Detroit to help the protest for Black civil rights, is shot and killed by Ku Klux Klansmen as she drives toward Montgomery to pick up a carload of marchers. She was thirty-nine.

- August 6, 1965—President Johnson signs the Voting Rights Act into law.

MY ENTRY ON THIS timeline began in late 1964. At that time, Martin determined that SCLC should most likely make Selma the focus of our voting rights effort in Alabama. As director of national affiliates, my job was to see if that city of about thirty thousand population (today, about eighteen thousand) and the surrounding environs would welcome our involvement. Why Selma? For one thing, the Black population, led by the indomitable Amelia Boynton, Marie Foster, and the Reverend Frederick Douglas Reese, was clamoring for the right to vote. And let's be honest: Selma was home to a virulent, racist sheriff, Jim Clark, a beefy World War II veteran and cattle rancher, who often dressed in military garb and carried a cattle prod. Clark—who wore a button that proclaimed his timetable for integration, "NEVER"—was almost certain to respond less than peacefully to our peaceful initiatives. We needed a conflict that would demonstrate our plight and the fact that the establishment did not respond with indifference but with violence. Such a response, we hoped, would sicken Northerners as Birmingham had and motivate an already sympathetic President Johnson to expedite voting rights legislation.

SNCC had already been in Selma for a couple of years. Its goals and strategies, however, differed from ours. Briefly, SNCC favored a grassroots organizing effort aimed, admirably, at developing strong local leaders and an empowered citizenry to press for a wide range of changes. Understandably such an effort takes time and doesn't always offer the sizzle that attracts media attention.

SCLC, on the other hand, came to town to use nonviolent direct action to mobilize public opinion and influence lawmakers—in this case to achieve voting rights. Attracting media attention was paramount to this undertaking. The people of Selma wanted Martin because he would garner that attention while leading a well-organized, strategic drive.

Frankly, I don't remember where I was every day during those first three months of 1965. I do remember being in Brown Chapel for Martin's speech on January 2. In fact, I had helped set it up.

As you may know, January 1 is Emancipation Day; it's so named because it commemorates that the Emancipation Proclamation went into effect on New Year's Day, 1863. We would have liked to inaugurate the campaign on January 1, 1965, but it so happened that another event had drawn Sheriff Clark and other city leaders out of town for the day: the

University of Alabama football team was playing the University of Texas in the Orange Bowl in Miami. We wanted Clark in town because we figured there was a good chance he'd make mass arrests since the meeting would be in violation of Judge Hare's injunction about gatherings of more than three people.

As it turned out, Sheriff Clark was still out of town on January 2, and the marginally more tolerant local Director of Public Safety Wilson Baker did not arrest the hundreds of area residents who filled Brown Chapel and the street outside. No matter. It was important that Martin was there. Wherever we went in those days, whatever promises we made, until Martin actually showed up and laid out the plan, the locals were skeptical.

On this night Martin did not disappoint. "We must be willing to go to jail by the thousands," he told the crowd. "We are not asking, we are demanding the ballot." He added that the United States faced a critical question: could democracy "exist for her twenty-two million Black children."

Over the next weeks, we organized several attempts to demand the ballot at the Dallas County Courthouse, and Clark ordered the arrest of well over a hundred of us. If you saw the 2014 movie *Selma*, you may remember a scene in which the fabulous Oprah Winfrey—portraying the equally fabulous fifty-four-year-old Annie Lee Cooper—was confronted by Clark on the courthouse steps. Mrs. Cooper and others had been waiting in line for hours to register when Clark ordered them to go home. He punctuated the order by pushing her with his cattle prod. Mrs. Cooper, who weighed more than two hundred pounds, responded with a right hook to Clark's jaw. The punch knocked him to the ground, and she was quickly arrested.

Fast forward about two weeks to one of the most important days in my life—and, many say, in the life of the Selma campaign. On February 15, 1965, I led about forty local Blacks intent on registering on a half-mile march from Brown Chapel to the courthouse. Clark, his deputies, and a handful of television crews were waiting for us.

Before continuing with this story, let me say this about Jim Clark: He was a bully, but he was hardly unique. His society, his culture allowed bullies. Look at the values that the churches they went to taught. You can't be good under those circumstances. Understanding this, you won't be surprised to learn that Clark not only denied our contingent of would-be registrants entry to the courthouse, but his manner was, shall we say, less than friendly or polite.

I didn't punch him as Ms. Cooper had—at least not literally. But I did go for the gut, asking: "What do you tell your wife at night? What do you tell your children?"

No answer. My memory of what followed has been greatly aided by a 2013 article in the *Atlanta Journal-Constitution* by the talented reporter, Ernie Suggs. When the sheriff turned away, I kept up the verbal jabs, saying: "You can turn your back on me, but you cannot turn your back on the idea of justice. You can turn your back now and you can keep the club in your hand, but you cannot beat down justice."

Clark wasn't the only one trying to beat down justice. As was usually the case, local Whites had gathered to lend their support to law enforcement. And as usually was the case, their imaginations and vocabulary were less than impressive. "Screwball," someone yelled.

My response: "I'm a screwball for the rights of people to vote, and if this is the kind of screwball I am, this is the kind of screwball America needs—the kind of screwball that can get rid of Sheriff Clark, who beats people on the streets and keeps people from registering to vote."

Apparently the Whites found this funny. "You're laughing because you don't know what else to do. There was a day when you would beat me instead of laugh, wouldn't you?" I said.

Then to Jim Clark: "There was a day when you would arrest everybody and say, *Well, we took care of that.* But the day of your criminal activity is just about over, gentlemen, and you're going to have to survive by the means of law and order."

No answer.

Then to the sheriff's deputies: "We want you to know, gentlemen, that every one of you, we know your badge numbers, we know your names."

As Suggs reported:

Clark finally spoke, asking Vivian if he lived in Dallas County. Vivian said no, but he represented county residents who could not vote. Vivian turned and faced the crowd, taking them to church with a call and response.

"Is what I am saying true?" he yelled.

"Yeah!" the crowd responded.

"Is it what you think and what you believe?" Vivian asked.

"Yeah!" they shouted.

Clark finally snapped. He ordered the TV cameramen to turn off their cameras. "If you don't turn that light out, I'm gonna shoot it out," Clark barked.

The deputies started pushing the marchers down the stairs, as Vivian pleaded to them not to beat them. Clark then punched Vivian square in the face with a vicious left jab, sending him sprawling down the court-house steps.

I was hurting but brushed myself off and rose quickly. I remembered the training I'd received from Jim Lawson in Nashville. We can never allow violence to defeat nonviolence. You have to resist the impulse to turn in the other direction and leave. You have to stay. Leaving is the last thing you want to do. If you turn away, what are you gonna tell the people on the line with you?

It was important for people, Black and White, to understand the mean-ing of what we were doing. We had a right to be there. We had a right to vote, and here was the evil force that was stopping that.

It becomes very clear that we can never allow evil to destroy the forces of righteousness, even when beaten down. I had to get back up because otherwise people would have been defeated by violence. We can never allow violence to defeat nonviolence. There can be no questions unan-swered; the depth of the human consciousness must be told.

"You can arrest us. You can arrest us, Sheriff Clark." I said. "You don't have to beat us. "If we're wrong, why don't you arrest us?"

A policeman said, "Why don't you get out of in front of the camera and go on. Go on."

"It's not a matter of being in front of the camera," I said. "It's a matter of facing your sheriff and facing your judge. We're willing to be beaten for democracy, and you misuse democracy in this street. You beat people bloody in order that they will not have the privilege to vote. You beat me in the side and then hide your blows. We have come to register to vote."

Suggs wrote: "Because it was carried on television, historians have called Clark's attack on Vivian one of the defining moments of the civil rights movement. 'He knew it was gonna advance the movement the instant it happened,' said Taylor Branch, the Pulitzer Prize-winning author of several histories of the civil rights movement."

The confrontation did not surprise me, but my words did. When I started that day, I had no idea what I was gonna say; I wasn't even thinking about that. I just knew when the time came, I would say something. I had no idea it would be that great. But it just kept coming out, almost as though I was in the courtroom. It's a mystery when those things happen, and they don't happen that often. I've already mentioned one other time: when the guard pulled the gun on me at Parchman Farm.

With Jim Clark, it was a clear engagement between the forces of the movement and the forces of the structure that would destroy the movement. It was a clear engagement between those who wished the fullness of their personalities to be met, and those that would destroy us physically and psychologically. You do not walk away from that. This is what movement meant. Movement meant that finally we were encountering, on a mass scale the evil that had been destroying us on a mass scale. You do not walk away from that, you continue to answer it.

It does not matter whether you are beaten; that's a secondary matter. The only important thing is that you reach the conscience of those who are with you and of anyone watching—both the so-called enemy, and those who are preparing the battle, and anyone else who may be watching.

I'm flattered that my dear friend Andy Young told Suggs: "No one gave C. T. any instructions to do that. It took a lot of courage to get in Jim Clark's face. But if he had not taken that blow in Selma, we would not have had the Voting Rights Act."

If you are so disposed, you can watch a portion of this confrontation online. Google "YouTube C. T. Vivian Jim Clark confrontation in Selma 1965" and you'll see several links to filmed snippets.

CLARK'S ORDER TO ARREST me was not exactly music to my ears, but I didn't mind being taken into custody. Being arrested meant we'd have to go to court. Remember, when he knocked me down I said, "You don't have to beat us. Arrest us." I knew he didn't want to do that. Why take the chance of losing in court when you can beat people so you can say, "Well, nobody said that anything was wrong."

My experience in the Dallas County Jail also called to mind Parchman. Every now and then over the years, I'd encounter a policeman who was so big he looked like he should have been playing for the Chicago Bears. A cop in the Selma jail fit that bill. When he and I and the head jailer got in the rinky-dink elevator to go up to where the cells were, I knew what was going to happen.

"Let me hit him," the cop said to the jailer.

The jailer looked at him as if to say, "You're sick." But he didn't say it. He couldn't say anything. See, one of the things you learn—and you don't have to be in the Deep South, and you don't have to be in jail, and you don't have to be between policemen—is that the hardest thing for a White man to do is to tell another White man he's a racist.

The jailer turned his head, and when he did, I knew it was coming. I tried to get my fingers together, and just as they came together, the blow came down. My fingers gave a cushion, and that cushion made all the difference in the world. Had I not got to this position, that cop could have really hurt me.

Not that I wasn't hurt. I had padded the blow to my head, but I couldn't feel the ends of my fingers for quite some time. It took three days for the pain to stop in my hand. They ended up taking me to Good Samaritan hospital—the one hospital in Selma that took in Black people.

Sadly, Good Samaritan would soon admit another Black man, Jimmie Lee Jackson, who had suffered injury at the hands of a White law enforcement officer. As John Lewis once observed, Jimmie Lee's "blood and death gave us the Voting Rights Act of 1965." True. Here's the short version of the story you can find in books such as *Jimmie Lee & James: Two Lives, Two Deaths, and the Movement that Changed America*, written by my collaborator, Steve Fiffer, and Adar Cohen. The "James" in the title is James Reeb.

A little background: Marion, a town then of about three thousand, about thirty miles northwest of Selma, is often overlooked in histories of the civil right movement. But it played a central role in our battle for the right to vote. In rural towns such as Marion, Black men and women were often reluctant to openly join the cause. Why? Because many either sharecropped on the land of White folks or were employed directly to work on the farms or in the homes owned by White folk. Involvement in the movement—even an action like trying to register to vote—could easily result in losing one's livelihood. Still, Marion—under the leadership of Albert Turner and the Perry County Voters League—had a more active community than most in the Alabama's Black Belt.

The movement there received a huge boost in February 1965 thanks to a strategic move. At that time, SCLC's man on the ground, James Orange, organized high school students to leave their classes and sit-in at local segregated establishments. Eventually many students and some adults as well were arrested and carted off to a detention farm near Selma. Conditions there were terrible. One toilet. Sandwiches that contained rat feces. Yes, rat feces!

The arrest and mistreatment of these brave youngsters caused many of their parents to come off the sidelines and join in protests and the voter registration cause. Then on February 18, Orange was arrested in Marion for contributing to the delinquency of minors. His alleged crime had nothing to do with sex, but for persuading the students to leave school without permission.

Almost immediately after the arrest, a protest was planned. The community was to gather at 7 p.m. at the Zion United Methodist Church on the town square. After songs and speeches, the crowd would then exit the church in threes and march peacefully to the nearby jail where Orange was being held. Mind you, nighttime marches were rare. The police were often emboldened to assault us in plain daylight. Imagine how much they relished the opportunity to attack us under the cover of darkness.

I was barely out of jail and the hospital following my run-in with Jim Clark when the folks in Marion called and asked me to give the main speech at the church. Activist Willie Bolden would also be speaking. At the time SCLC staff based in Atlanta was taking turns manning the Selma office. Because I was in charge on this day, I told those in Marion I'd have to return right after speaking. I wouldn't be able to march.

Initially, I really wasn't too worried about something happening in Marion. Although any nighttime march presented peril, the chance for violence here was somewhat mitigated because the march would be short. Also, the media had been alerted and would be present and bear witness.

I didn't know that state troopers were gathering in Marion. I didn't know that the police chief had deputized local White vigilantes. I didn't know that Jim Clark had driven over from Selma. I didn't know that there were rumors Clark was interested in going after a Black man this night—and that man might be me because of our earlier confrontation. And when I left the church via the back door to drive back to Selma after speaking to the four hundred men and women who had assembled, I had no idea what was awaiting them minutes later.

As the assembled slowly filed out of the church for the march, they were met by the police and ordered to disperse. The Reverend James Dobynes, who was at the front with Albert Turner and Willie Bolden, knelt on the sidewalk and asked if they could pray. And then?

Suddenly the lights on the street went out, and the police and troopers began their assault. A trooper clubbed Dobynes on the head. Another trooper put his gun in Bolden's mouth and threatened to kill him. Police, troopers, and vigilantes also went after the fifty or so others who had thus far made it out of the church. They also attacked the press, beating reporters and photographers so the atrocities couldn't be documented. NBC reporter Richard Valeriani had to be hospitalized.

Some of the marchers tried to get back inside the church. Some hid under cars or in doorways. And some took refuge in nearby Mack's Cafe.

The troopers followed them into this popular eatery and bar. Jimmie Lee Jackson heard his eighty-two-year-old grandfather, Cager Lee, had been injured and ended up in Mack's looking for him.

Eyewitnesses would later say that Jimmie Lee saw his mother struggling with a trooper, attempted to help her, was shot, ran out of the café, collapsed on the street, was kicked by police or troopers, and was finally taken to the local hospital, where he had to wait for attention. Requiring more sophisticated care, he was then sent to Good Samaritan in Selma.

Martin visited the young man in the hospital. Initially, it appeared Jimmie Lee might recover, but he took a turn for the worse. He died on February 26. The trooper who shot him, James Bonard Fowler, claimed he had acted in self-defense. Not surprisingly, the local all-White grand jury refused to bring charges against Fowler.

At a rally on the day Jimmie Lee died, elderly Marion voting rights activist Lucy Foster said they should carry the casket from Marion to Montgomery and place it on Governor Wallace's doorstep. And that, my friends, is when the idea for a march from Selma to Montgomery was born.

I HAD MY OWN misadventure the night Jimmie Lee was shot. After leaving the church, we were going down the hill towards the highway to Selma when we saw police cars coming up the hill heading into Marion. *What's going on?* Then, when we got near the intersection that runs into the road to Selma, I saw a big policeman standing with a flashlight directing the police cars where to turn. *What is this?* I hesitated, thought about it, and decided to go back up the hill to Marion.

When I got back to town, Zion United was dark and empty. So I went to Hampton Lee's funeral home a few doors down from the church to find out what was going on. Hampton, a longtime civil rights activist, told me that the police had attacked the marchers. I hurried back to SCLC headquarters in Selma. Later, the police came looking for me at the funeral home. In the days that followed, rumors circulated that Jim Clark and the state troopers planned the attack with one goal in mind: to get me. And if they couldn't get me? Get another Black man.

They got Jimmie Lee Jackson.

On March 15, four days after the White minister James Reeb died after being beaten by segregationists on the streets of Selma, President Johnson addressed the nation. "We have already waited a hundred years and more. The time for waiting is gone," he said. He called on the Congress to join him to work "long hours, nights and weekends if necessary to pass this [voting rights] bill." He closed the speech by saying, "And we shall overcome."

I watched the speech with Martin and others in Selma at the home of a black dentist and his wife, Dr. Sullivan and Richie Jean Sherrod Jackson. As the president spoke, there was celebration everywhere. Most of us were jumping around. I looked over at Martin, and he was just sitting there, rather staid. He was just sitting in his chair, and a tear started to roll down his face.

Later in the evening Martin talked to LBJ on the phone. The following day he told the press that the president had shown a "great and amazing understanding of the depth and dimension of the problem of racial justice . . . We are happy to know that our struggle in Selma has brought the whole issue of the right to vote to the forefront of the conscience of the nation."

Martin would later reflect on one omission in Johnson's address: "In his eloquent 'We Shall Overcome' speech, [the President] paused to mention that one person, James Reeb, had already died in the struggle. Somehow the President forgot to mention Jimmie Lee Jackson, who died first."

A POSTSCRIPT:

In 2005, Dallas County District Attorney Michael Michael Jackson reopened the investigation into the death of Jimmie Lee Jackson (no relation). In 2010, former Alabama State Trooper James Bonard Fowler, by then seventy-seven years old, pled guilty to manslaughter and was sentenced to six months in jail. The irony was not lost had it not been for the efforts of Jimmie Lee Jackson and others who won the right for Blacks to vote, the African American Michael Jackson would never have been elected to his position.

Three years later, on June 25, 2013, the U.S. Supreme Court gutted the 1965 Voting Rights Act in the case, *Shelby v. Holder.* In the 5–4 decision, the Court opined that because past discrimination had abated, key provisions of the law were no longer necessary. In a fiery dissent, Justice Ruth Bader Ginsburg wrote: "Hubris is a fit word for today's demolition of the VRA. . . . One would expect more from an opinion striking at the heart of the nation's signal piece of civil rights legislation."

Those of us who fought for voting rights couldn't have agreed more. John Lewis called the decision "a dagger into the heart." Speaking of the five conservative Supreme Court justices, he said: "These men never stood in unmovable lines. They were never denied the right to participate in the democratic process. They were never beaten, jailed, run off their farms or fired from their jobs. No one they knew died simply trying to register to vote. They are not the victims of gerrymandering or contemporary unjust schemes to maneuver them out of their constitutional rights."

I can only add that everybody on the Supreme Court knew exactly what the Voting Rights Act did and continued to do. Those four White men and one Black man in the majority knew their decision would destroy what we had worked for, what some had given their lives for.

7

The Disease of Racism

Our struggle for voting rights, for all of the human rights systematically denied us, continues. In states with significant Black and Hispanic populations, Republican-controlled legislatures—emboldened by *Shelby v. Holder*—conjure new means for suppressing registration and voting. The Supreme Court ruled that states may continue to gerrymander districts for political purposes. President Trump's Commerce Department proffered the bald-faced lie that it needed to put a citizenship question on the U.S. Census so that it could enforce the Voting Rights Act. In fact, as a memo later revealed, inclusion of the question was designed to dilute the political power of non-Whites. This ended up becoming one of the rare instances in recent years where the increasingly conservative Supreme Court ruled in favor of the people.

Meanwhile, President Trump repeatedly revealed his racist self by tweeting and then doubling down on abhorrent, dangerous lies about four congresswomen of color. In addition, the U.S. Department of Justice determined that it would not bring criminal charges against the police officer who put Eric Garner into the chokehold that led to another unnecessary death of an unarmed Black man or child. See: Tamir Rice, Michael Brown, Philando Castile, et al.

Am I surprised by any or all of the above? Absolutely not. I was under no delusion that passage of the Voting Rights Act of 1965, as monumental as it was, would make the world right. The same goes for the election of Barack Obama in 2008. After Selma in 1965, we all knew that there was a great deal of work that needed to be done.

Here's what I was thinking: *You may have won something, but you're not going to hold onto it without strong leadership. And good leadership comes from good training. To take advantage of our newly achieved right to vote and to implement necessary change once our folks are voted into office, we need a new generation of young, educated Black leaders in the South.* Figuring out how to develop this *new* leadership for the New South was essential. Otherwise the old guard would come back, the potential for a new order would disappear, and it wouldn't be too long before we didn't have anybody at the top.

In my capacity at SCLC, I was interacting with all the affiliates. As a result I knew the strengths and the weaknesses of our people, knew that we needed more and better training. We had a lot of young men and women with enough nerve to go to jail, with enough understanding and depth to withstand whatever was thrown at them. Now they needed to be back in school.

Many of them had been expelled and were not being reinstated. So, how could we get them *back in* and get a lot of other kids *into* college? Same thing with respect to Black kids that had dropped out of school because their heroes and role models—Black teachers, principals, and administrators—had been summarily demoted or fired by Alabama and other states. As the Pulitzer Prize–winning *New York Times* columnist Brent Staples has observed: In the years following *Brown v. Board of Education*, "When Black schools were shuttered or absorbed, celebrated Black principals were demoted or fired. By some estimates, nearly a third of African American teachers lost their jobs. Those who survived the purge were sometimes selected on the basis of a lighter skin color that made them more palatable to White communities."

Disheartening, right? So here was my idea to get every deserving kid, particularly every deserving Black kid, to college: Step One: Design a program that would allow all of these young people to pass high school exams so they could go to college. Step Two: Raise whatever money was necessary to help them go to college.

I CALLED IT "VISION." Some others called it "Vivian's Vision." There were plenty of young people who wanted to participate in Vision. To help them pass exams, we needed teachers, tutors. We put the word out, and a lot of talented students from some of the best colleges in the country agreed to come to Alabama to work with our kids. These prospective tutors wanted to be part of the movement, just as others had been during the Freedom Summer effort in 1964–65. You know the saying, "Ask and ye shall receive." Well, I asked the people in charge of the Iowa Test for copies, and they gave me all I wanted. Pass that test and you could show you were college-ready.

If you want to see a copy of the first pamphlet for the "Vision Alabama Tutorial Project," you can visit the website of the Low Country Digital Library. You'll find that our initial sponsors were SCLC and the St. Louis Conference on Religion and Race. During the summer of 1965, we offered two successive six-week tutorial sessions in ten Alabama cities and towns. Allow me to quote from the pamphlet:

We first articulated our analysis of the present day:

After the bitter feelings and the strong emotions of people have been expressed, the problems of our generation are still with us. There are few people who could deny that all Americans who are of age and of sound mind should be able to cast a vote in elections. But it is true as well that most Americans recognize the importance of a responsible electorate and the continuing need for responsible leaders.

Next, we listed our goals:

To prepare high school students (grades 9–12) for college entrance.
To find the level of advancement of each interested student and tutor him to his proper level of intellectual achievement.
To awaken within each participating student an appreciation of learning.
To properly prepare Negro high school students for integration of high schools and colleges.
To lay the basis for year-round tutorial participation and a scholarship program.

We noted that the students would answer to college and university tutors directed by professors working with local high school teachers. The tutors would receive twenty dollars per week and housing, and a teaching space would be provided.

Churches were encouraged to sponsor tutors. We also got help from the folks running the education component of President Johnson's Great Society program. I was able to get them to send tutors to every one of the cities and places that we had our students going.

Aware of safety concerns, we differentiated between protest and educational activities. We assured prospective tutors and students: "This is an all-day, every-day program. No one participating in VISION will be engaged in any action programs at all."

I didn't have control over any money. But Martin had given me the go-ahead to do anything I wanted to with the program. He didn't monitor the effort; I just gave him a report at the end of the year. No surprise that he was happy with our progress, as he had always appreciated the importance of education. I believe he graduated from grade school, high school, even Morehouse, ahead of time.

I've been blessed to receive a great deal of recognition over the years for my activities. I'm always surprised that more attention isn't paid to Vision. We placed more than seven hundred young people into colleges, with scholarships. And even if you haven't heard of Vision, you may have heard of the program it morphed into, "Upward Bound." Among the alums of that ongoing program: Oprah Winfrey, the actresses Angela Bassett and Viola Davis, political strategist Donna Brazile, and basketball Hall of Famer Patrick Ewing.

WHILE OFFERING BLACK STUDENTS in Alabama and elsewhere the opportunity to go to college, many of us realized that the South was not the only region of the country that required our attention and fresh leadership. The *de facto* segregation and economic disenfranchisement in Northern cities could be just as devastating to our people as the discriminatory *de jure* policies in the states below the Mason-Dixon Line.

Early in 1966, Martin and I each moved to Chicago. He and SCLC, including Jim Bevel, Al Raby, and Bernard Lafayette, birthed the Chicago Freedom Movement, while I became involved with an initiative started by the Urban Training Center (UTC). I lived on the South Side of Chicago for the next four years. Let me tell you how that came about.

Not too long after Selma and the founding of Vision, I received a phone call from the Reverend Jim Morton, director of UTC, asking me to join him in Chicago. Here's a good description of UTC provided by the University of Illinois-Chicago, which administers the organization's papers:

The Urban Training Center was an ecumenical institution, founded in 1962, devoted to the training of clergy and laity for Christian mission in the metropolis. Reverend Donald Benedict first proposed the idea for establishing a training center in Chicago whose staff would consist of representatives affiliated with several denominations. James P. Morton was the director of a staff that included Richard Luecke, J. Archie Hargraves, Carl Siegenthaler, Paul Kraemer, Niles Carpenter, and Stanley Hallett. The founders of the UTC believed that the Church had lost relevance in a modern, urban society, as it catered primarily to the affluent White middle class, whose values were reflected in the modern Church. Ignorant of the circumstances of the urban lower classes, the Church needed to develop new strategies of outreach into the urban environment. Its pedagogical method was rooted in the principle that for the Christian, the key to the understanding of the urban problem is participating in the structure and dynamics of that problem in every facet. Participation in urban life would facilitate a new theological relationship of the Church to society. The purpose of the UTC was to expose its interns to as many realities of the city; immersion in the various communities was a key first step to understanding the multitude of issues facing those living in American cities. These institutions functioned into the 1980s, when a lack of funds forced their closure.

Sadly, few people know about this organization. It's not an exaggeration to say that we remade the Christian church. That was necessary. The National Council of Churches had come to the realization that it had to reform a model largely based on serving the agrarian community. Based on my travels to SCLC affiliates and my speaking engagements across the country, so had I. The new world was now urban, and most of the churches were unprepared to minister to the urban poor and disenfranchised.

Most of the churches, but not all. The Black churches were ahead of the curve. Martin was a great example. He had moved the effort from the South to Chicago. At UTC, my job would be to bring more Black ministers and laypeople into the fold for training. Why me? Jim knew that as SCLC's director of national affiliates, I'd been involved in training folks across the country and had the right contacts.

Jim, an Episcopalian in his mid-thirties, was quite a guy. This 1964 press release from the Diocesan Press Service does a good job of summing up the man and the mission:

A man of diverse interests and talents, Father Morton graduated Phi Beta Kappa from Harvard University with a degree in architecture. But two years of post-graduate study at Trinity College in Cambridge, England, and a chance to study the worker-priest movement in France reversed his career directions and he returned to New York for theological study at General Theological Seminary. There he added a Bachelor of Divinity degree to two BAs and a Master of Arts degree, the latter two obtained at Trinity College, Cambridge.

As director of Chicago's Urban Training Center, Father Morton will coordinate an experimental, cooperative venture that initially will involve more than three hundred clergy and laymen from all over the country. The program, to be launched in September, has the support of twelve major American churches and will provide an ecumenical training ground for clergymen, seminarians and laypersons interested in metropolitan mission.

Father Myers (Jim's predecessor) has carved out a year-round curriculum that ranges from four to thirty-six week stretches. He has warned prospective candidates that participation in the program will be both "intense and brutal." An example of this is a five-day "exposure period" for students to discover what it is like to be hungry and jobless. They will be turned out on Chicago's streets and forced to forage for themselves, either by finding a job or by begging at church or social agencies. In addition to the problem of unemployment, students also will deal with political action, racial conflict, juvenile delinquency, and other social issues that hang over the nation's 220 sprawling city centers.

Although I'd been envisioning an effort similar to UTC, I was initially reluctant to accept the offer. UTC planned to have ministers from around the country come to Chicago for one to three months of training. "That won't work," I told Jim. "No matter how committed, no Black minister can leave his church for that long. I won't be able to get any takers."

After some thought, I proposed a variation on the theme. "I'll take the job if you take the money you've set aside for the ministers' weekend room and board and other expenses and give it to them so they can travel back and forth to their home churches to preach on the weekends." Deal. And thanks to the Ford Foundation, we eventually ended up with hundreds of thousands of dollars for a variety of expenses.

After settling into Chicago, I began bringing ministers and seminarians in for training. The goal was for them to get trained and then go back to their home cities and work with other UTC people. That way we'd have a good nucleus to serve the needy.

I remember bringing virtually an entire seminary to Chicago for a month so they could understand what was happening in the urban world. Many would eventually decide that they wanted to be the person that represented the new urban church for their denomination.

The first UTC had been in New York. Then Chicago. Later Atlanta. Before it ended, more than twenty centers around the country were doing work we hadn't seen before. In Raleigh, North Carolina, for example, UTC alum started two housing projects.

For an in-depth look at UTC, I direct you to a recent paper by Professor Erik Gellman, formerly of Roosevelt University in Chicago, "Faith in Black Power: Chicago's Urban Training Center for Christian Mission, 1966–1970." Doesn't the following Abstract make you want to know more, especially its reference to "the Plunge"?

How did Chicago's denominational churches engage with the Black freedom struggle in the late 1960s? Founded in 1963 by several local churches "transcending denominations," the Urban Training Center for Christian Mission (UTC) represented one such response. I will explore how the scale of UTC programs changed dramatically with the award of a five-year grant from the Ford Foundation to train African American pastors and organizers. The subsequent appointment of C. T. Vivian as Director of Fellowships and Internships in 1965 took this program in an explicitly political direction. (Jesse Jackson was among the first nineteen men trained under Vivian's program at the UTC in 1965.) By 1968 Vivian and others designed two sessions of Chicago Action Training (CAT) at the UTC for planning a strategy of Black Power, Black identity, and Black unity because, according to the UTC, "Black CATs are no longer hung-up on services; they see the taking of power from structures which affect their lives."

Students who came to the center attended lectures, read history, discussed strategy, and engaged in innovative training exercises like "the Plunge" where participants had to survive on their own for seven days without access to housing, food, or other resources. By analyzing the combination of religious, Black nationalist, and other ideologies that formed the basis of the UTC's pedagogy in the late 1960s, this paper will then seek to understand how activists applied their training in different protest groups on the West and South sides of Chicago, especially compared to other religious and civil rights groups like the Community Renewal Society. Moreover, the UTC's history has the potential to illuminate new dimensions of late 1960s protest movements in Chicago, bringing a reevaluation of activist networks and goals, the ideology and practice of Black Power, and the role religious faith played among its participants.

I'D BEEN IN CHICAGO for about two years when Martin was assassinated on April 4, 1968. It was one of the worst days of my life. I heard the news on the radio while driving home. "Are you going?" Octavia asked when I walked through the door. I nodded and began packing. Soon, my friend Pastor Charles Billups—an often forgotten hero of the movement—and I were on a plane to Memphis. When we arrived, we went with several others to pick out the casket.

There was a wake at the R. S. Lewis Funeral Home, and then Martin's body was flown to Atlanta on a plane chartered by then U.S. senator and presidential candidate Bobby Kennedy. Two months later, he, too, would be assassinated.

Before I left Memphis for Atlanta, I went to the Lorraine Motel and stood on the balcony of Room 306 where Martin had been shot. Then I went across the street to a rooming house where the assassin had apparently fired the shot. It was haunting, wrenching. Martin, so young, had meant so much to so many. My emotions were roiled soon after when I watched the newly widowed Coretta view the casket for the first time.

In the years that followed my good friend's death, I found myself doing a great deal of thinking about him—as a man, a movement leader, a prophet. My conclusion? Though he lived just thirty-nine years in the middle of the twentieth century, Martin Luther King Jr. was a twenty-first-century man. I put on paper some of my thoughts about this in 2007 when I wrote the Afterword to a new edition of *Letter from Birmingham Jail.* Those thoughts—adapted to reflect even more thinking in recent years—appear in the next chapter.

MEANWHILE, FOLLOWING MARTIN'S DEATH, riots occurred in many cities. Soon parts of Chicago were literally on fire. Out of the ashes arose CUCA—Coalition for United Community Action.

Mary Lou Finley, Bernard Lafayette, James R. Ralph Jr., and Pam Smith edited a fine book, *The Chicago Freedom Movement: Martin Luther King Jr. and Civil Rights Activism in the North.* Here's a portion of their interview of me. Note the involvement of Chicago's notorious gangs and the notorious gang leader Jeff Fort; this was revolutionary.

So the city burns down (after MLK) was killed, and we come down to a meeting to see what we're going to do with this. We joined together with a number of men that were heads of major businesses like Sears and Roebuck, Wards, First National Bank, and Continental Bank—about thirteen guys.

After the town was just about burned down, they wanted to create something and make a difference. So I came in with the plan that we create something for the South Side. Archie Hargraves wrote it up, but I laid it out for them. We created a plan for a whole organization. We needed about $8 million, so that had to come from the businesses downtown. (Later we saw that the $8 million could come from the federal government.)

We brought together sixty-one non-governmental organizations and formed the Coalition for United Community Action. But the real players, the big-time players, were the gangs. Our concern was how do you move from their usual way of thinking? If you could get them involved, then they become the force you need to go after the biggies. If you don't have any force that's not already bought by city hall or the businessmen, what force are you going to use to change Chicago?

This is where we came in. We gathered together another group which we called the Roundtable. The Roundtable was made up of Black adults that everybody could appreciate who worked downtown in the big companies as vice presidents and things like that. By the time we had everything going smoothly, the gangs came to the position that if any of their guys got in a fight with another, what they would do is ask for these community leaders. They became kinds of uncles to the group. We created a group that made decisions so that the gangs wouldn't have to shoot each other and fight each other all the time. We would decide who was right and who was wrong.

The first thing we did was close down the Red Rooster stores. They were all over the South Side of Chicago, and they sold bad meat, or nearly bad, and bad vegetables, at the same price as if they were good. So we wanted to stop those Red Rooster stores from selling bad stuff. Jeff Fort, head of the Blackstone Rangers, had people working at the Red Rooster, so he pulled his people out and demonstrated with us at the Red Rooster. This was one of the things that connected us with the gangs.

The YMCA also had someone working with the gangs, and he said he wanted to meet me and we had an evening of it. We needed the power of the really poor and left-out to be the force that would demand jobs from the city in spite of city hall. What do you have to break into to show that these young men are an important part of the city and got jobs?

The building trades unions had all kinds of jobs, but if you were Black you didn't become a full member of any of them. So we had to take on the unions. We organized demonstrations at the building sites. We were confronting them. We weren't just standing there looking at them and saying we're hungry. We were saying, "You're not giving us jobs, so it's time you get out of here."

We did it nonviolently, but all those guys in the union were afraid; we weren't. They would leave work, and the work would stop. We stopped half a billion dollars of work right downtown in the middle of the city!

The mayor (Richard J. Daley) called me and said we needed a meeting. We met at city hall because nothing was going to happen unless the mayor said it was going to happen. Monsignor Egan was my friend, and he knew the mayor very well. We finally convinced the mayor that I wasn't against Chicago; I was for Chicago. And little by little he came to settle it. We were talking about union jobs where we would demand not only the wages but the union cards to go along with it. It was called the Chicago Plan. And later that became the Boston Plan, the New York Plan, the Newark Plan. It moved all over the country. In fact the national administration had to come our way.

We got the twenty thousand jobs and the administration gave us the money; five thousand jobs a year for four years, four thousand jobs a year for five years. You can only win in Chicago once, and here we did. We won.

If you want to know more about this period, I can point you to a couple of good resources: 1) "The Rise and Fall of the 1969 Chicago Jobs Campaign: Street Gangs, Coalition Politics, and the Origins of Mass Incarceration," an entry in the *University of Memphis Law Review* Vol. 49, by Toussaint Losier; and 2) a chapter by the aforementioned Professor Gellman in the book, *Black Power at Work: Community Control, Affirmative Action, and the Construction Industry*, edited by David A. Goldberg. I should add that both writers rightly point out that the establishment worked very hard to prevent the concessions we extracted from being implemented and, in some cases, succeeded in maintaining the network that prevented Black participation. This was disappointing to all of us, but we were heartened by the progress we did make and the demonstration that involving the gangs could make a difference. No one was surprised that the powers that be tried to hold onto their power despite the promises they made. That game plan has always existed and exists today.

A few more things about my time in Chicago:

While there I had positive relationships with folks whose names may or may not be known to you. Remember, Martin was living on the West Side as the Chicago Freedom Movement took hold. Jim Bevel, Al Raby, Albert Sampson, Jesse Jackson, Bernard Lafayette, Charles Billups, to name but a few, were either involved with that initiative and/or other efforts in the city. Meanwhile the Reverend Arthur Brazier (whose church I attended) and Saul Alinsky started The Woodlawn Organization (TWO). Saul tried to recruit me for TWO, but despite our friendship I chose to remain with UTC.

Also while there, my book, *Black Power and the American Myth*, was published by Fortress Press in 1970. Here's how the publisher described it:

C. T. Vivian stands in the forefront of the new struggle for Black equality. The civil rights movement failed, says Vivian, because it was based on certain myths about America—like the myth that legislation would lead to justice. The explosion of these myths has changed strategy and tactics, but the goal of Black equality remains. This . . . candid analysis of the Black Movement . . . was written to help the bewildered White man understand and to give the Black man an articulate statement of his case.

Before I quote a few passages to give you a sense of what I was arguing, I have to tell you that I was not the top-selling author in the Vivian household. That honor deservedly went to Octavia, who wrote the first biography of a dear friend: *Coretta: The Story of Coretta Scott King*. Now a few passages from the second-bestselling Vivian book:

The United States began with a struggle for civil rights . . . the American colonists decided that this oppression was not tolerable. They began to protest: first by petition, then by demonstration, and when they proved futile, by armed revolt. America was born as a revolutionary nation.

This is the American heritage: the struggle for freedom, the striving to build a land with liberty and justice and . . .

That sentence must remain incomplete. Freedom liberty, equality, and justice are truly parts of the democratic inheritance, but this is an inheritance which we have never fully claimed, for it is inextricably bound to another—the legacy of slavery.

After fifteen years of struggle, the wall of ignorance, superstition, intolerance, and violence remains. And now the movement is taking on a new direction. . . .

Having assumed that integration would be the principle of our success, we accepted the corollary proposition that the basic hindrance we faced was legal segregation. We therefore directed our efforts to removing the laws which limited us and to creating new laws which would set them free, but as these things were in fact accomplished without bringing the freedom we sought. We began to see that we were dealing not with a legal matter but with a sickness, the disease of racism, this is the problem to which our energies must now be addressed. . . .

One measure of both our success and our failure is the cycle of rebellion and repression which has now become common in almost every city. Our success is seen in the changed expectations of Black people. Our failure is defined by the unchanged list of horrors that describes the Black condition. . . .

But today, in the minds of most people, the nonviolent movement as we once knew it is over. New strategies are emerging. . . . The most intense "activists" of the Movement are no longer singing of brotherhood on freedom rides through the South. They are coldly preparing underground networks and stockpiling arms and ammunition for urban guerilla warfare in the North. . . . This mood must be accepted and taken seriously by the White community, for it is already taken seriously by the Black. . . .

A revolution is in progress here. Only the *kind* of revolution is in question. The time for choice has arrived. And it is not choice that the Black community can make. The Black community can only respond to the forces directed at it from the larger community. A real change of style and content which takes Black needs and Black demands seriously will increase the possibility for peaceful coexistence. Continued repression will strengthen the forces of revolt. . . . People do not choose rebellion; it is forced upon them. Revolution is always an act of self-defense. . . .

The time is gone when we can deal with anything but the most fundamental issues. The days of tokenism, accommodation and co-option are gone. We must begin to engage the basic splits in our nation. And only to the extent that we deal realistically with these issues will we be able to meet the crisis of our times. . . .

Right now the day of our own judgment has arrived.

Reader, I wrote these words fifty years ago. I leave it to you to determine how relevant they are today, how much has changed in the last half-century.

8

Prophets Never Stop Serving

As promised in the previous chapter, here are some extended thoughts about Martin King, a movement leader, a prophet, and a thoroughly twenty-first century man.

THE BASIS OF ALL human rights today is the result of a movement that moved all of us. In fact, the lives and lifestyle of almost everyone in America today, regardless of color, was formed or decided by their action, or reaction, to the civil rights movement as led and declared by Martin Luther King Jr. For most of those in the South, past or present, Black or White, our incomes and education and religion have been affected and improved by the movement. Martin's movement was the beginning of the transformation of America—a true transformation of America and the American Dream.

Those of my generation and those who grew up in the 1960s can't help but know something of this great man and his deeds. Those who weren't alive when Martin was assassinated in 1968 study him in school and know he did something important enough to get a holiday named after him—though not without a too-long delay. But all too often I come across young men and women with little or no knowledge of Martin. It saddens me but no longer surprises me. Subjects we should be studying closely are often observed only through the rearview mirror. And sometimes—driven by the need to come up with something new or shocking—these observations sully or distort the view, reducing our ability to see the big picture.

As someone fortunate enough to have known Martin from the mid-1950s until his death in 1968, to work side by side with him, to laugh and to weep with him, I'm often asked to provide a perspective on the man

09

and the movement he created and led. In 2007, I did so for the Afterword of a lovely special edition of *Letter from Birmingham Jail*, illustrated by the extraordinary African American artist Faith Ringgold and published by the Limited Editions Club. I titled my remarks: "Martin Luther King Jr.: 21st Century Man." I've changed some of the words around here, but not my thinking.

My thesis was simple: Martin became America's greatest social strategist by taking the Bible in one hand and the Constitution in the other, and then turning them on America like a mirror. He used these two great documents that undergird the laws, thought, and principles of this nation, and made America take them seriously. Speech after speech, one direct action nonviolent confrontation after the other, changing one law after the other, in one state and then another, he made Americans face who they really were.

Nonviolent direct action helped us to free ourselves and others at the same time. Even those who did not think of themselves as involved were freed from evils of the spirit they could not see or acknowledge. This peoples movement forced the most powerful nation in the world to say "yes" when it wanted to say "no," and it empowered passive bystanders to energetically join the freedom chorus. Together they forced America to admit that it was a sick society.

The movement put America's mind in conflict with its mythical self and helped it regain a path to sanity. Martin made the people of this nation ask a basic question, "Who am I?" Moreover, to ask the basic philosophical question, "What does it mean to be human in my own time?" And, "What is my nation's belief system, and does it reflect the person I choose to be and what I want my family and neighbors to become?"

THERE WAS AN AMERICAN world before Martin. But, it was a mean, cruel, ugly, and distorted world. Multi-millions were encouraged to feel superior, by making millions of others feel inferior. Every institution in American life was used to damage, destroy, and discourage the mind, the will and the psyche of anyone who was not White. The darker you were, the greater the degree of your punishment.

Those of us who suffered from racism realized that racism destroyed more people physically and psychologically than any other factor in American society and had been doing it longer. And while we had little or no reason to believe America would ever end its racism and our suffering, we never lost hope. The African American national anthem, "Lift Every Voice and Sing," declares in song what we endured when "hope yet unborn had died."

Martin realized America was sick on greed. For hundreds of years its White citizens had used men, women, and children as things to be bought and sold at will. This was true from the first president of the nation, to the man who wrote that "all men are created equal," to the lowest social level of White man who could scrape together enough money to buy one slave or rent a slave for a season. A racist nation allowed such men to be in charge of human life and sit in church pews, praying to God. Few ever asked for forgiveness.

Martin saw this nation as sick on violence, too. He saw the violence inside our borders as well as in our involvement in wars around the world. He saw the interaction between the two and realized America's life style could never bring peace, at home or abroad. "The ultimate weakness of violence is that it is a descending spiral begetting the very thing it seeks to destroy. Instead of diminishing evil, it multiplies it," he said.

He saw the result lead to two world wars and had spiritual reason to believe it would lead to a third thanks to Vietnam and the deployment of our troops in permanent locations across the world. He saw millions of people in jail, more than in any other country in the Western world. Well over half of these were African American, Latino, and poor, uneducated White persons. He saw and decried the lack of social agencies and programs to change the lives and conditions of persons while in prison or when returned to the streets.

SO WHO WAS THIS special man with the intellectual and spiritual depth to give oppressed people a sense of dignity and personal worth? To change a nation?

The son and grandson of ministers, Martin graduated from Morehouse, the finest college for Black men in America. After entering Morehouse at the tender age of fifteen, Martin found an intellectual father in the college's president, Benjamin Mays. A scholar, national speaker, author, and educator, Dr. Mays weekly stood in the front of the Morehouse Chapel where every man had a numbered seat. When Dr. Mays did not speak, he had the finest black thinkers, intellectuals, ministers, leaders of Black America, Black college presidents, and successful Black persons in every field speak to the audience. A faculty of educators—brilliant in their own right—taught the students daily.

Upon graduation with a BA in Sociology in 1948 at age nineteen, Martin entered Crozer Theological Seminary in Pennsylvania, an institution known for its modern theological and philosophical thought. He stood out in this atmosphere, becoming a fine preacher and student and senior class president. Martin had a deep devotion to nonviolence and, from the very beginning while in seminary, he began to form his profound philosophy of nonviolent direct action and plan its application to America.

Reading Gandhi and studying at seminary, he said, "I came to see for the first time that the Christian was one of the most potent weapons available to oppressed people in the struggle for justice. Jesus Christ furnished the spirit and motivation while Gandhi furnished the method."

After Crozer, Martin moved on to Boston University, where he continued to excel and received his doctorate in 1955. A favorite among his professors, he founded the Dialectical Society, which helped to create a bond among the few African American students. The group met monthly to discuss philosophical and theological ideas in relation to the African American condition in the United States. (That group would later come to his aid in various cities and help to lead his organizations. Wyatt Tee Walker, whom he met while preaching and lecturing at various colleges and seminaries, later became executive director of SCLC.)

Martin was "called" to ministry. Despite his family history, he initially fought the idea of being a minister and the image of the average minister of his time. As time passed, however, he obeyed God's calling as understood by the African American community. It was not until he had received his doctorate and was pastoring in Montgomery and was chosen by his community to lead the movement that the deep meaning of the call came to him.

The epiphany came after Martin received a series of abusive phone calls. Finally, after a middle-of-the-night call threatening his family, he prayed aloud to God. According to his wife, Coretta, he sought strength and guidance. "I am at the end of my powers. I have nothing left. I've come to the point where I can't face it alone." As he considered the ways he might best protect those he loved and lead the people who had come to depend on him, he heard a still, small voice, the voice of which the Bible speaks. It said, "Stand up for righteousness. Stand up for truth. And God will be at your side forever."

His mind comforted and his philosophy validated by the highest power, Martin would later explain: "The method of nonviolent direct action was one of the most potent weapons available to the oppressed people in their struggle for freedom."

Alabama was central to Martin's strategy to move us forward by a tactic previously foreign to American soil. He consciously chose one of the most backward states in our nation as the battleground to prove that nonviolent direct action could free a people, indeed, a nation. He did with Alabama what the colonists did with Massachusetts—turned it into a test laboratory. The three most important cities of the movement were Montgomery, Birmingham, and Selma—all in Alabama.

Montgomery. During the famous Rosa Parks-triggered bus boycott from December 1955 to December 1956, fifty thousand African Americans marched out of their churches led by the ministers who decided to follow Martin and put their trust in nonviolence. Soon, entire African American communities joined the movement. A year of walking and organizing taxis and personal cars into a carpool that daily delivered people to work, shopping, and churches made victory possible.

African American lawyers trained in the nation's best universities, supported by the ministers, students, and the masses, finally caused the Supreme Court to rule in their favor. The united, determined, resolute, creative, African American people of Montgomery won against all odds.

Most important was that Montgomery proved the efficacy of

nonviolence. Within a few weeks, many cities began organizing to gain similar freedoms. Millions of African Americans came alive as in no time since leaving their native lands and entering this country almost four hundred years earlier. After the Montgomery victory, Martin was invited into every major pulpit and public forum to speak to overflowing crowds of all races; a novelty in those years.

Five months after the boycott ended, SCLC brought people from across the nation by train, bus, and plane to protest in Washington, D.C. At "the Prayer Pilgrimage," the right to vote was a major theme. "Give us the Ballot," with no strings attached, Martin demanded.

I've already chronicled the SCLC initiatives—all of them nonviolent — between this event in 1957 and Selma in 1965: the Albany Movement in 1961; Birmingham in 1963; St. Augustine in 1964. The Birmingham Crusade was instrumental in pushing Congress to pass the civil rights Act of 1964. And Selma, of course, did get us the ballot with passage of the Voting Rights Act. Massive action on the world stage—where the villains were plainly the states and their agents, not the protesters—led to landmark laws. Martin understood this and effectively organized the masses on a national scale.

But it was not just the masses. Martin also had to convince many preachers and moral activists as well as persons who lived by violence and others who lived under violence that an alternate path to meaningful power existed. In so doing, he had to educate many and inform others to offset the attacks against the movement.

Some followers wondered if power and love could be wed harmoniously, Martin told them, "There is nothing wrong with power when it is used correctly." He did not always convince every listener. But he did have the capacity to make difficult ideas simple. He went on to say, "Some of our philosophers get off base. And one of the great problems of history is that the concepts of love and power have usually been contrasted as opposites, polar opposites, so that love is identified with resignation of power, and power with a denial of love."

He continued: "It was the misinterpretation that caused the philosopher Nietzsche to reject the Christian concept of love. It was this same misinterpretation that induced Christian theologians to reject Nietzsche's philosophy of the will to power in the name of the Christian concept of love."

Martin was able to explain such difficult concepts in Black church mass meetings as well as in halls of learning. "What is needed," he explained, "is a realization that power without love is reckless and abusive, and that love without power is sentimental and anemic. Power at its best is love implementing the demands of justice, and justice at its best is love correcting everything that stands against love. This has led African Americans in the past to seek their goals through love and moral methods devoid of love and conscience."

Martin's unassailable logic and unparalleled speaking ability invariably led to applause. After the applause, when he felt his audience understood, he would often apply philosophy and theology to practical problems. "Such thinking is leading a few extremists," he said, speaking about the call for Black Power, "to advocate for Negroes the same destructive and conscienceless power that they have justly abhorred in Whites. It is precisely this collision of immoral power with powerless morality which constitutes the major crisis of our time."

He did the same thing on every social issue. "The movement," he said, "must address itself to the question of restructuring the whole of our society. There are forty million poor people in America, and one day we must ask the question, 'Why are there forty million poor people in America?' When you begin to ask that question, you are raising a question about the economic system, about a broader distribution of wealth. When you ask that question, you begin to question the capitalist economy. I'm simply saying that more and more, we've got to begin to ask questions about the whole society. We are called upon to help the discouraged beggars in life's marketplace. But one day we must come to see that an edifice which produces beggars needs restructuring."

Racists and conservatives confronted by his vision of society and his call for systematic and structural changes would often accuse him of being a communist. "Communist" was a scare word—a little like "socialist" today—seldom understood by those who used it.

Whenever the question of communism came up, Martin would answer much as he did in the midst of the Poor People's campaign in 1968. "Communism forgets that life is individual. Capitalism forgets that life is social. And the kingdom of brotherhood is found neither in the thesis of communism nor the antithesis of capitalism, but in a higher synthesis, that combines the truths of both."

Martin always had more to say than was first presented to an audience. When pushed he would suddenly reach back and speak of the philosophers who brought him to that conclusion. "I did not get my inspiration from Karl Marx, my inspirations do not come from Engels or Trotsky or Lenin," he said. He told the audience he had read *The Communist Manifesto* and *Das Kapital* "a long time ago." He said that maybe Marx didn't follow Hegel enough. He took his dialectics, but he left out his idealism and his spiritualism. Marx went to a German philosopher named Feuerbach and took his materialism and made it into a system that he called "dialectical materialism." Martin made his position clear by saying, "I have to reject that."

Martin became involved in civil rights because he saw it as a necessary first step, but not as an end in itself. He realized American problems were too deep to be solved by law. He knew this nation, with its deeply individualistic and materialistic base, would never obey a piece of paper.

Martin was preparing our nation for the twenty-first century. Before he died *half a century ago*, he changed from being a strictly civil rights person to the next level—human rights. It had always been there in the broadness of his experience, but the point of change was never stated.

At the time of Martin's death on April 4, 1968, he had gone around the country and met with the leaders of other minorities and other peoples' movements. He was laying the groundwork for SCLC's Poor People's campaign. It was not only designed for minorities, but for White Americans. Poor Whites came up from Mississippi and places like it to join the Poor People's campaign. He structured the campaign and was involved in it as a human rights issue, not as an issue of racism only. Racism always had to be central to Martin's work, until as a major issue it was overcome. However, near the end he was clearly showing us the need to go beyond racism and see our work as human rights.

We each moved to Chicago in 1966 to pursue different projects. One night after attending a dinner together, Martin turned to me. (I should preface what follows by explaining that he had his own way of bringing up a subject or desiring to bounce ideas "off-the-wall" as a way to think through whatever was on his mind.)

"Vivian," he began, "you probably think I don't know what I am talking about on this Vietnam thing!" At first, I was a little hurt that he thought so; but that feeling left quickly. As we continued, he brought up many of the ideas that he later used in his famous Riverside Church speech of April 1967. He went from the statistical facts to the levels of suffering of the Vietnamese people. He saw the violence destroying the people's lives and their way of life. He spoke of the abject poverty and our soldiers, our military, our pesticides destroying thousands and thousands of acres of the Vietnamese homeland. We Americans were the cause of the people's poverty and hunger and death, the prostitution, shame, loss of heritage and self-worth. Somewhere in the midst of his reflections he discussed the policies that caused the suffering, destruction and death of "more than flesh," and the continuing spiritual effect on our citizens and national decisions.

When I got to the hotel, I found it hard to sleep. However, I was certain that we were moving beyond racism as we had known it. We would always, from this point forward, have an international perspective, and poverty would be written more indelibly on our minds. This was all before the Poor People's campaign.

The Riverside Church speech was not universally acclaimed. Martin's usual critics and those who supported the war were, of course, critical. But so, too, were many of his followers who thought he should—to use a twenty-first-century term—"stay in his lane." Stick to fighting racism in the U.S., the NAACP said, not the fighting in jungles half a world away. The *Washington Post* editorialized that the speech had "diminished his usefulness to his cause, his country, and to his people."

It was Martin's speeches and faith in nonviolence that became the force that caused millions of all faiths, and races, to rise up and particularly throw off the yoke of racism, and also join the anti-war organizations.

Those same qualities made him America's greatest and most effective people's movement leader. It was his superior education, personal suffering, and deep commitment to end racism and all social injustices that made his natural talents effective.

He reached the moral and spiritual core of the nation. The nation was forced to struggle with its idealized image of America versus the stark reality of its daily existence. They were also made to see their so-called innocence as passivity. Martin became the conscience of our nation.

His was the voice of a new beginning for America. It was the voice of freedom and it spoke in various ways. His outspoken truths and his love of even "the least of these" caused people to speak out and act on behalf of themselves and others. We could hear it coming from elderly women in Montgomery who chose to walk to work rather than ride a segregated bus and be daily demeaned. We could hear it from Mississippi, where a judge stood before a young pregnant activist who with her husband listened to the judge's threat, "If you don't agree to end protesting Mississippi law your child will be born in jail." She quickly replied, "Wherever my child would be born in Mississippi it would be born in jail." Young White people came forward to join and be led by Blacks like themselves. Ministers of most all denominations marched to win victory over a basic American evil.

Martin's greatest gift to average people regardless of race, color or class was a means of settling social problems without violence. So many movements followed the civil rights movement. The Women's movement was revived. The Youth movement began. The Brown and Red movement became a force in the atmosphere created by Martin's movement. The Gray Panther movement saw a relationship, and though the elderly were never violent they took on the spirit of the Panthers.

Just prior to Martin's death, one of the world's greatest rabbis, Abraham Joshua Heschel, introduced Martin to a conference of rabbis. He said, "Where in America today do we hear a voice like the prophets of Israel? Martin Luther King is a sign that God has not forsaken the United States of America. God has sent him to us. His presence is the hope of America. His mission is sacred, his leadership is sacred, and his leadership is of extreme importance to every one of us. Martin Luther King Jr.

is a voice, a vision, and a way. The whole future of America will depend on the impact and influence of Dr. King."

After Martin's death I became interested in the attributes and characteristics of those known as "true prophets" and began to study the works of those who gave their lives to the study of prophets. I found several characteristics that stood out and Martin met each of them. For example, true prophets never manipulated others or circumstances to be chosen for leadership. They became leaders chosen by their followers.

When Mrs. Rosa Parks sat down on the bus, Martin did not rush forward to speak of his PhD in theological studies, or his knowledge of nonviolence. Rather, after Mrs. Parks was released from jail, the leaders of the movement called a meeting, elected him president of the Montgomery Improvement Association, and asked him to address the community at large. Martin had less than an hour to prepare for what became a memorable speech. After he finished, the assembled rose as a body in support of this charismatic young minister. It took 382 days, but under Martin's leadership, the cause was victorious.

My studies revealed many objective factors seen in the lives of prophets that fit Martin's life. Prophets create radical changes in their culture. Often, they guide their generation and set patterns for generations after them. They put nations on track. Their leadership lets people know how to live. Most importantly, the lives of prophets allow a people and a nation to actually see and know the possibilities of their own humanity in their time.

Prophets never stop serving people. They are often martyred, as were the disciples. They are not driven by a desire for material things and often set the necessary goals for a faltering nation and delineate the issues and methods a nation must follow to thrive under God. Martin was all of these.

Martin, like so many prophets of their own times, was tested by God. The personal threats he received in Montgomery evolved into realities when his parsonage was bombed. Some in the community wanted to respond to this violence by taking up arms; they believed that White people had not the decency to ever love or care for anyone but themselves and people of their own color and would use force to maintain power. This act of trying to kill the King family was proof.

Martin passed the test of the prophets by telling the people to put up their weapons. He talked to them about nonviolence being God's way and asked them to go to their homes. That was a harbinger of things to come. Martin was ready to represent his God in a world of violence and racist criticism from every side. Martin never met violence with violence.

As I've noted, my wife, Octavia, authored the first biography of Coretta Scott King. At a birthday party for Octavia, Coretta told several of us that on the day of the bombing, she and a neighbor who was holding the Kings' first child, born only weeks earlier, were chatting in the living room. Suddenly, she recalled, she had an intuition of danger and told her friend, "Let's move to the kitchen." She said she did not go to her kitchen her regular way, but moved there rather rapidly by a different route. Immediately, the bomb went off near the room they had just left.

The prophet of our times, who became the most important and celebrated person in the most powerful nation in the world, left us with his agenda for the future. He moved the nation further in a shorter length of time than any other person in our history. His method of organizing people for nonviolent direct action rooted out racism and taught us how to finish the task. The prophet who brought us this far in the transformation of America left us an agenda and guidelines for the future before the opposing forces martyred him at the age of thirty-nine.

Martin entered his active ministry at a church literally across the street from the Alabama Capitol later presided over by Governor George Wallace, the South's chosen leader to deny equality to African Americans. Even after Martin's death, the two forces of segregation and liberation, with their starkly opposing values, struggled at the local and national level.

For us to fulfill Martin's vision he felt it necessary to share his revolution of values. He realized to some extent, as did his religion's Founder, one cannot put new wine into old wineskins. Martin King and the great Martin Buber agreed that a revolution of values demanded that we move from a thing-oriented culture to a person-oriented culture.

Martin's revolution of values included personal compassion and individual moral change but also demanded structural change. "True compassion is more than flinging coins to beggars, it understands that an edifice that produces beggars needs restructuring," he said.

My friend also saw that it was nothing but a lack of social vision and shortsightedness that prevented us from reordering our national priorities, so that the pursuit of peace could take precedence over the pursuit of war. A revolution of values meant that our loyalties should become ecumenical rather than sectarian.

Before Martin was assassinated, he outlined the tasks for the twenty-first century and beyond. They were the end of racism, the end of poverty, the end of war. He called them the triple evils.

Studies often show something mysterious about prophets. Martin passes that test, too. Shortly after the bus boycott he wrote his first book, *Stride Toward Freedom: The Montgomery Story.* During a book signing in New York, an African American woman leaned over the chair where he was signing and asked him if he were Martin Luther King Jr. "Yes ma'am," he replied kindly.

She plunged a letter opener into his chest. The blade stopped just short of his aorta. The *New York Times* reported that had he sneezed he would have died. The mystery was not in the stabbing. It was to come afterwards but not to be publicly revealed until his death.

Immediately after the rifle shot rang out in the semi-darkness of the Memphis night at the Lorraine Motel, Martin was rushed to the hospital. His tie was cut off and his shirt was ripped open. Doctors saw a cross over his heart.

It was not a metal cross on a chain. It was made from his own flesh. Years earlier, when the New York doctors removed the letter opener, they made short cuts on each side of the downward stroke of the blade so it could be carefully withdrawn. Later the cuts healed into a cross covering his heart. He very seldom spoke of it. Those of us who knew realized that every day he lived with the reality of death at any moment. It was also a message to us, his followers: *Ours is a dangerous but necessary task, that must endure until death.*

Martin understood from the beginning the purpose of his calling. On the window of the SCLC office, he wrote: "To Redeem the Soul of America."

9

What Do You Want to Be?

Collaborator's Note: In his final months, Dr. Vivian was unable to complete this manuscript telling the story of his remarkable journey. The second half of his life—post-Chicago until his death on July 17, 2020—was devoted to, as he wrote, "engaging the basic splits in our nation." This chapter detailing some of the highlights of this period is based on previously recorded interviews.

In 1972, THE REVEREND Archie Hargraves, then the president of Shaw University in Raleigh, North Carolina, invited Dr. Vivian to become dean of alternative education in the divinity school at what is the oldest historically Black university in the South. The two men had known each other in Chicago, during the UTC days. At Shaw, Dr. Vivian, with funding he secured through the Lilly Endowment, implemented the experimental phase of a concept he had personally developed—the Seminary Without Walls (SWW). This was a system of independent, off-campus study that offered the bachelor of theology and master of divinity degrees.

It was through SWW that Dr. Vivian met Don Rivers, who would become his professional associate and best friend until Dr. Vivian's death. In 1974, Rivers, then in his early twenties and a producer for radio station WBT in Charlotte, North Carolina, came to Shaw to interview with Dr. Vivian for the position of SWW audio director. "We had an instant spiritual connection and camaraderie," remembers Rivers. "I recall that he had a statue of a train on a railroad track on his desk that said, 'You can be on the right track, but if you just sit there you will get run over.'"

Rivers was hired on the spot, given a budget to build a complete recording studio, and subsequently oversaw the recording of lectures by top theologians and academics including Lerone Bennett and Drs. Vincent Harding, James Cone, Ben Jochannan, and John Gibbs St. Clair Drake.

Students across the country listened to these recordings remotely and then came to Shaw to be tested. After passing all their courses, they would receive their theology degrees.

Rivers remembers:

Seminary Without Walls operated out of Meserve Hall, which was a three-story mansion that formerly served as the housing for the past presidents of Shaw University. Dr. Vivian traveled from Atlanta to Raleigh on Mondays and back to Atlanta on Fridays when he was not traveling around the world. When he was in Raleigh, he would stay in Meserve Hall. When I moved to Raleigh, Dr. Vivian invited me to stay in the attic.

I lived in the attic about one month, then moved into an apartment complex that had great amenities including swimming pools and tennis court, thus providing us with various activities to stay fit. Whenever he was in town, Dr. Vivian would stay with me.

We worked long hours and to unwind we would run four miles, play tennis, swim, or listen to jazz music. We did at least two of these activities every day.

I looked forward to him being in town because I had never met anyone who was so dynamic and spiritual. I was twenty-one and could not believe that a fifty-one-year-old gentleman had so much energy and grace. I became a sponge as I observed how he genuinely cared about the human race. For example, I was driving Dr. Vivian to a meeting. It was storming and the rain was pouring down. We came to a stop sign and an old White gentleman who looked to be homeless walked in front of the car in the crosswalk. Dr. Vivian put his head in his hands and burst out crying. I asked him what was wrong and he raised his head with tears running down his face and said, "I wonder what brought this gentleman to this point in his life." This is but one of many indelible memories of Dr. Vivian's caring nature that I cherish. Dr. Vivian was a gentle, courageous, no-nonsense man and loved all living things and had no barriers.

Dr. Vivian lived by principles that I attempt to live by on a daily basis which are "Truth, Ethics, Respect, Justice and Love." He was about the People, the Community, and Serving. He lived a life of unselfishness and never looked for or wanted any recognition. He truly lived by the Greek word *Agape*: giving unselfishly without looking for anything in return. These experiences were the basis for our lifelong friendship.

For the last fifteen years of Dr. Vivian's life, I primarily handled all of his business and traveled with him all over the world. I would not have traveled and met all the beautiful and spiritual people that I have if it was not for me being Dr. Vivian's humble servant and friend. The world is a better place because of Dr. Vivian. It's like a part of my heart is gone because I loved him so much. I am missing him still, tremendously.

In 1977, Dr. Vivian founded Black Action Strategies and Information Center (BASIC), the nation's oldest consulting firm dealing with the management of a multiethnic workforce. Initially designed to help develop policies and strategies to foster diversity and understanding, the company now focuses on best practices for inclusion under the leadership of Dr. Vivian's son, Al. BASIC has conducted workshops and training sessions for many of North America's major corporations, nonprofits, educational institutions, and governmental agencies.

Dr. Vivian in 2015:

That's a decision I really had to make. Now that the movement is over, what am I going to do? There's only one thing I really care about, continue to get rid of racism in the land of the free and home of the brave. So I started doing workshops, and I have the best workshops in the nation.

When people went through our workshop they never forgot it. Because it grew out of people who were deeply concerned about getting rid of racism, not how much money they made.

My son Al eventually took over for me. He'd been in the military and was ready to go to the next level. But then he saw me talking about the workshops on the Oprah Winfrey Show—first time anyone had been on her show two days in a row. He saw it and decided not to re-up and came home, and said, "Teach me." And now he's better than I am.

In 1979, along with Anne Braden, Dr. Vivian co-founded the National

Anti-Klan Network in response to renewed bigotry and the resurgence of violent white supremacists. This coalition, which evolved into the Center for Democratic Renewal, began as a network of more than sixty civil and human rights groups concerned about the resurgence of violent bigotry against individuals because of their race, sexual orientation, religion, ethnicity, and national origin. The network also worked closely with interfaith and religious institutions

In 1984, the Reverend Jesse Jackson asked Dr. Vivian to help him in his campaign for the presidency. Dr. Vivian signed on, becoming national deputy director for clergy. Dr. Vivian in 2016:

I just closed down my real workshops, right, for six months to help Jesse. Now I knew he wasn't going to win, but that wasn't the point. And what I was about is that anybody who wanted to run—any Black person who wanted to run for president—I wanted to help 'em.

Jesse came over right after [bringing back the hostages from Iran] and said, "Could you be at the meeting with me tonight? Because I want you—I am running, and I want you on my staff."

So I did, and week after week after week, I was going somewhere to sell, sell Jesse and answer all the questions that people had, right. And I always have thought deeply about it. I wasn't happy about everything that happened, but I really wanted to do anything I could to help at all.

The story that stands out for me: a woman in Atlanta said that she always—right after Christmas, she would ask the kids, "What do you want to be?" And this is the first time anybody said, "President of the United States," two, two black guys. And that was worth my going up and down the country.

Dr. Vivian also campaigned for and counseled Barack Obama when he ran for the presidency in 2008. After Obama won, Dr. Vivian was at a meeting with the newly elected president, Michelle Obama, John Lewis, and a small group of black leaders. Dr. Vivian in 2016:

I got teary-eyed, right. And when he, when President Obama walked in. And see, what I was thinking about was we had Martin and now we had a president, right—and what will the next be? What could it be, right? But thanking the Lord, right, all the time. When you really think about how great all this is, that in a short length of time—and I didn't think we'd have a president for another hundred years. I really didn't.

In the mid 1990s, Dr. Vivian played a major role in assisting prominent Atlanta banker George Andrews in creating a Black-owned bank in Atlanta, Capitol City Bank and Trust, and at one the time served as chairman of the board. After twenty-two years of ups and downs, the bank failed. C. T. and Octavia Vivian invested their only savings in the bank. In 2015, he recalled:

We didn't have anything, but hey we can still love our neighbor. I was on the board of a bank. We put $100,000—only time we had one hundred grand—we put that into a bank because Black people in Atlanta needed a bank. You know what the wife said when I asked her about it—should we or shouldn't we?

She said: "We've put the little money we've had in the movement and everything that went with it. And the next great battle we'll have to have is income. Can people have enough to get a decent education, or are you just getting an education from those who control everything but you can't get anything because you don't have enough money to have an education for your children."

See, that's the point: do you love people enough—and my wife did. She said that we've got to fight the economic battles sooner or later and that people shouldn't have to be without simply because we haven't won yet.

It hurt me to lose the bank, but I didn't know enough, right. But we kept it open for twenty-two years. And a businessman called me and said, "Don't worry, Vivian. Don't let it hurt you. For twenty-two years you got to make certain that people who might not have started a business, people that may not have been done this or done that, were able to do it because you guys at the bank could loan 'em the money." Well, I really hadn't thought of it that way, but when I heard it, it made you feel so good.

In 2008, the C. T. Vivian Leadership Institute (CTVLI) opened in Atlanta with the assistance of Don Rivers and good friends Henrietta Antonin, Billye Aaron, and Dr. Bill Cleveland. This nonprofit organization is dedicated to the development and sustainability of communities. Dr. Vivian explained that he wanted to "create a model of leadership culture in Atlanta." CTVLI serves as a hub to centralize existing programs and services to work in coordination with local organizations to serve the needs of the community. The Institute is designed to create an atmosphere where lifelong learning can take place in all stages of life. The CTVLI focuses on four areas that are critical to the success of individuals and communities: Faith, Personal, Education, and Economic Development. CTVLI programs are designed to reach each participant wherever they are, with the goal of taking them where they want to be. By offering classes to the individual and services to the community as a whole, the specific needs of both will be met.

In 2018, it was announced that the C. T. and Octavia Vivian Library would be an integral component of an ambitious public space in the Vine City neighborhood of Atlanta, not far from Dr. King's home and the new Mercedes-Benz Stadium. Named after a White politician who long advocated for civil rights, the sixteen-acre Rodney Cook Sr. Park will feature eighteen monuments to civil rights leaders and a 110-foot tall peace column. A museum within the column will be anchored by the Vivian Library. The library's board was formed with the help of good friends George and Janice Andrews and the Reverend Gerald Durley and attorneys Michael Coleman and Andrew Patterson.

Though the Library will be new, its "occupants" will not. Dr. Vivian's love of books has already been mentioned. As a young man he began collecting nonfiction and fiction written by (and about) Black men and women. At his death the collection numbered about six thousand volumes—the majority of which resided in his home in southwest Atlanta. He was delighted that the public at large would be able to access the books, which are tangible testaments to the literary talents and intellect of African Americans and deal with subjects important to the Black community and community at large.

The collection includes first editions from W. E. B. DuBois, Langston Hughes, and Ralph Ellison. One prize: a signed second edition of the collection's oldest book, Phillis Wheatley's *Poems on Various Subjects, Religious and Moral*. Written in 1773, this is the first known book written by an African American woman.

There are also works by Dr. Vivian's favorite poet, Claude McKay. The Harlem Renaissance luminary's 1921 poem, "America," resonates one hundred years later:

Although she feeds me bread of bitterness,
And sinks into my throat her tiger's tooth,
Stealing my breath of life, I will confess
I love this cultured hell that tests my youth.
Her vigor flows like tides into my blood,
Giving me strength erect against her hate,
Her bigness sweeps my being like a flood.
Yet, as a rebel fronts a king in state,
I stand within her walls with not a shred
Of terror, malice, not a word of jeer.
Darkly I gaze into the days ahead,
And see her might and granite wonders there,
Beneath the touch of Time's unerring hand,
Like priceless treasures sinking in the sand.

In January 2018, Dr. Vivian told *Atlanta Journal-Constitution* reporter Ernie Suggs, "We never thought the collection was valuable in a sense of money. . . . [but was] valuable in the sense that we can read our history. I want every Black child to be able to read about themselves. So books about Black people were always nearby for my children and for anyone who wanted to read about Black people and understand how we got this history."

Dave McCord, a prominent book collector and dealer who became a close friend, spoke at the funeral about Dr. Vivian's love of books:

Books, books, books. By love or serendipity, I was in his life when C. T. began collecting, and I was transitioning from collector to dealer. During those early years, I'll admit he kept my lights on a couple of times, if not more. But the real reward was to watch him look through every box of newfound books that I took to his house. They were immediately his new friends. Collectors: there all kinds of them, but there is a hierarchy. And C. T. sits at the top. He is the collector for whom the book is a tactile experience of what he loves and values. The book is not an option; it's an intimate relationship. His library is not a room for books; it's a place of rejuvenation, contemplation, and sanctuary.

At a recent board meeting for C. T. and Octavia Vivian's library, my dear friend C. T. looked at me and said, "I remember when we met." From a friend and hero, I couldn't ask for more. Our friendship had bonded over a love of history, a great deal of which he made, and at that time a love for the writings and poetry of Langston Hughes. I don't do spoken word very much anymore, but this one—Langston Hughes's "Dreams"—is for C. T.:

Hold fast to dreams
For if dreams die
Life is a broken-winged bird
That cannot fly.

Hold fast to dreams
For when dreams go
Life is a barren field
Frozen with snow.

For me C. T. was a dream keeper, always holding fast for dreams of the better world.

Epilogue

The Trail They Blazed

Dr. Vivian passed away peacefully at home at 3 a.m. on July 17, 2020, less than two weeks short of his ninety-sixth birthday. His daughter Kira was by his side. He was talkative until two days before his death and, even at the end, knew his family was there.

During his final two weeks, he discussed the resurrection with daughter Denise. "He smiled when I told him he'd see Mom and all of us again," she said. "This conversation occurred because he admitted to me that he knew he was dying."

Dr. Vivian also asked his daughter Jo Anna to tell him about home. She asked if he meant Peoria or Macomb, and he told her Macomb. Says Denise, "He loved Macomb."

It's probably no surprise that as death approached, Dr. Vivian asked Jo Anna to read "Amos," his favorite book from the Bible, to him. Amos 5:24—paraphrased by Martin Luther King Jr. in his "I Have a Dream" speech—was a cherished passage:

But let justice roll down like waters,
and righteousness like an ever-flowing stream.

UPON DR. VIVIAN'S PASSING, former President Barack Obama released the following statement.

Some thoughts on the Reverend C. T. Vivian, a pioneer who pulled America closer to our founding ideals and a friend whom I will miss greatly:

Today, we've lost a founder of modern America, a pioneer who shrunk the gap between reality and our constitutional ideas of equality and freedom. C. T. Vivian was one of Dr. King's closest advisors, a field general in

130

his movement for civil rights and justice. "Martin taught us that it's in the action that we find out who we really are," Reverend Vivian once said. And he was always one of the first in the action—a Freedom Rider, a marcher in Selma, beaten, jailed, almost killed, absorbing blows in hopes that fewer of us would have to. He waged nonviolent campaigns for integration across the South and campaigns for economic justice throughout the North, knowing that even after the Voting Rights Act and Civil Rights Act that he helped win, our long journey to equality was nowhere near finished. As Rosa Parks once said of Reverend Vivian, "Even after things had supposedly been taken care of and we had our rights, he was still out there."

I admired him from afar before I became a senator and got to know him as a source of wisdom, advice, and strength on my first presidential campaign. His friendship, encouraging words, and ever-present smile were a great source of inspiration and comfort, and personally I will miss him greatly. I'm only here because of C. T. Vivian and all the heroes of the Civil Rights Generation. Because of them, the idea of a just, fair, inclusive, and generous America came closer into focus. The trail they blazed gave today's generation of activists and marchers a roadmap to tap into and finish the journey. And I have to imagine that seeing the largest protest movement in history unfold over his final months gave the Reverend a final dose of hope before his long and well-deserved rest.

Due to the Covid-19 pandemic, Dr. Vivian's funeral on July 23, 2020, at Providence Missionary Baptist Church in Atlanta, was private, with only family and a small number of friends in attendance. Among the invited were Don Rivers, George Andrews, and Dave McCord—all of whom offered personal reflections. Also present were Atlanta Mayor Keisha Lance Bottoms and the children of several of Dr. Vivian's fellow movement leaders: Martin Luther King III, Michael Julian Bond, John-Miles Lewis, and Karen Lowery, who sang "The Lord's Prayer."

On the day before the funeral, a memorial service was held for Dr. Vivian in the Georgia State Capitol. In the tradition of other civil rights heroes, a horse-drawn carriage carried his casket to his friend Martin Luther King Jr.'s tomb.

The *Atlanta Journal-Constitution*'s Ernie Suggs reported:

Outside the church, a small group of fans of Vivian sang gospel songs, including "This Little Light of Mine" and The Impressions' "Amen." They held photos of Vivian above their heads along the street to let passersby know whose funeral had garnered so much attention as media swarmed the outside of the church.

Edna Davis brought her granddaughter Y'Habei Huggins with her to the church to say goodbye to C. T. Vivian. Davis, 65, wanted to make sure she let others know of his greatness. "We loved Dr. C. T. Vivian," she said. "He was very warm and friendly. He did not meet a stranger."

When her daughter Danielle was in the tenth grade, he welcomed her into his home for an interview as part of a class assignment. "Dr. Vivian was a quiet sort of man except when he got riled up because he needed to be," Davis said. "I appreciate the fact that he was willing to give his time and his life at such a young age. What I regret is that because he was quiet he was oftentimes overlooked."

The funeral was officiated by Dr. Vivian's daughter-in-law, the Reverend DeAna Jo Vivian, and was live-streamed over several Atlanta television stations. Those present or watching heard Reverend Vivian note that C. T. Vivian carried a list of one hundred books everyone should read. They also heard her husband, Al Sampson, say: "How do you adequately say goodbye to the greatest person you have ever known? A man who has been your father, your mentor, your frat brother, and still your friend after being your boss? The man who bestowed on me my witty, my sons would say corny, sense of humor? No matter how long I love, no matter whatever I accomplish, the greatest thing I will ever be known for is the son of C. T. Vivian." Another son, Mark, and son-in-law Andre Thornton also spoke.

Several prominent friends and admirers, including Joe Biden, also delivered remembrances via prerecorded video. These remembrances can be found in Appendix 1 along with portions of the Reverend Gerald Durley's stirring eulogy.

Dr. Vivian and his dear friend and fellow nonviolent warrior John Lewis died within hours of each hour. Together in Nashville, Mississippi, Selma, and so many other battlegrounds, the two were—for a brief period—also together in death.

Before their respective funerals, the two men lay side by side in identical closed caskets in the legendary Willie A. Watkins Funeral Home in Atlanta. Watkins, the mortician who had also arranged the funeral service of Coretta Scott King and others in the movement, told *AJC* reporter Suggs, "They walked together, talked together, and strategized together. They took the beatings that others didn't and survived unafraid. God took them at the ages of ninety-five and eighty. And now here they are in the same room—together."

Watkins's brother, Darrell, told Suggs that at 3 a.m. on July 17, he received a phone call from Dr. Vivian's family telling him of the passing. Not too long after personally picking up the body of one of his heroes, Darrell Watkins received the call notifying him of Lewis's death. He picked up Lewis, too—and then:

"I took him past C. T.'s house. I took him past Joe Lowery's house, where I stopped and paused. I found my way down Martin Luther King and onto Ralph David Abernathy, where the funeral home is located," Darrell said. "All these men. All these great men."

The funeral book celebrating Dr. Vivian's life—divided into sections on Intellect, Courage, Family, Faith, and Mark—concluded with a 1919 poem by Dr. Vivian's favorite poet, Claude McKay:

IF WE MUST DIE

If we must die—let it not be like hogs
Hunted and penned in an inglorious spot,
While round us bark the mad and hungry dogs,
Making their mock at our accursed lot.
If we must die—oh, let us nobly die,
So that our precious blood may not be shed

In vain; then even the monsters we defy
Shall be constrained to honor us though dead!
Oh, Kinsmen! We must meet the common foe;
Though far outnumbered, let us show us brave,
And for their thousand blows deal one deathblow!
What though before us lies the open grave?
Like men we'll face the murderous, cowardly pack,
Pressed to the wall, dying, but fighting back!

Appendix 1

Because He Existed

As noted earlier, due to the Covid-19 pandemic, the funeral service for Dr. Vivian on July 23, 2020, was limited to family and a small number of family friends from the Atlanta area. As a result, several individuals unable to attend in person recorded video remembrances which were incorporated into the service. These follow, and after them are a remembrance by his good friend Dr. John Hallwas and excerpted portions of the eulogy by the Reverend Dr. Gerald Durley.

JOE BIDEN:

I'm so honored to be part of this celebration of Reverend Vivian's long life of purpose and meaning. To the family, from his children to his great-great-great-grandchildren, thank you sincerely for allowing me to join you today.

I was an admirer. It is not easy to grieve in public. I know from experience. It's not easy to lose a loved one who means so much to so many, but who meant the most to all of you. And C. T. was truly a remarkable man, a man whose physical courage was exceeded only by his moral courage, whose capacity for love overwhelmed incredible hatreds, whose faith in the power of nonviolence helped forever change our nation.

The number of times he faced down being drowned, being beaten, being reviled, only to stand up, straight as a ramrod, bloodied but unbent, and declare the truth that he saw so clearly. "You cannot turn your back on the idea of justice." You know, it's hard for most people to wrap their heads around this, just what a man he was, but in Illinois and in Tennessee, in Florida and Mississippi, in the North and in the South, C. T. was there fighting to turn us back toward justice. A soldier who refused to raise his fists. A preacher whose voice helped electrify a movement. A leader who inspired generations to join him in the ceaseless march of progress.

C. T. didn't waste a single one of the days God granted him. But we all know that C. T.'s spirit is going to continue to inspire us to fulfill his mission, a mission that remains unfinished. Our fight for racial justice, to state the obvious, is incomplete.

And C. T.'s memory now commissions all of us into service to finish the work of perfecting our union, to make sure every person can freely exercise their sacred right to vote, to bring us that much closer to our ideals of equity and justice for all.

C. T. has earned his rest, joining in eternity his beloved wife, Octavia, and his eldest son, Cordy. And for as deep as we are in mourning of his loss, I can't help but think there must be a great celebration in heaven today. A reunion of good and faithful servants, entering together into the joy of the Lord. Many of us continue to feel here on Earth the hopefulness, the purpose that infused C. T. throughout his life. May God be with you all during these difficult days. I'm so honored to be a part of this.

OPRAH WINFREY:

I remember back in the '90s doing a series of racial seminars with Reverend Vivian on the *Oprah* show. What an impact he made on that audience, mostly White woman at the time, gently yet passionately confronting them on their ignorances and their denial of racial inequality.

We spent several days filming what would later be edited for airing, and it was a privilege to witness his wisdom teaching in action. In his presence, we were always learning more about our country, about ourselves, of what it means to stand for what is right. He was a giant for justice.

Maya Angelou says in her poem, "When Great Trees Fall," that "When great souls die, / after a period peace blooms, / slowly and always / irregularly. Spaces fill / with a kind of / soothing electric vibration. / Our senses, restored, never / to be the same, whisper to us. / They existed. They existed. / We can be. Be and be / better. For they existed." Reverend C. T. Vivian. We are better, because he existed.

BERNARD LAFAYETTE:

C. T. Vivian had a rhythm to his message, and his rhythm was really like music. And as he continued to make his points, he always went in depth. That was the intellectual part of it. You could always draw from what he had to say, okay? Not just a repetition of, say, verses, but he had a tone to it. And I would describe his preaching as an echo from heaven. He was so enthralling in readings and books and that sort of thing. He had about easily three thousand books or more, you know. It could be six thousand. So yes, I do remember the writings and that sort of thing. And his wife, Octavia, she was very much involved as a you know, I'd say a librarian almost because she did a very enormous collection of books. . . .

ANDREW YOUNG:

I was so close to C. T. as I was to Martin Luther King and I don't know that I'll ever be lonely, for the memories and the presence of my brothers like C. T. Vivian . . . will always be with me. He was always a pastor; he was always a preacher—and a good one. And his motivation was always spiritual. He didn't want attention; he didn't want money. He only wanted to do God's will and bring out the best in these United States of America and its people, regardless of their race, creed, color, or national origin. He was always very physical-fitness oriented. I say my knees are bad, and his knees held up all the way for ninety-six years because he used to go over to Morris Brown and run up the steps of the stadium and walk down and then run up again to stay in shape. Well, he and Jimmy Carter are the only people I know that remained the same weight they were in college right on into the last days of their life. He never gained a pound and he never lost his physical fitness. And he never lost his mental fitness, even in these last days, when a week or so ago I talked to him. His voice was weak but his thoughts were clear.

HENRIETTA ANTONIN:

When I think of our young men, how C. T. Vivian must have framed our young men, and given them the foundation, I'd like them to think about the life of Dr. C. T. Vivian and how he handled himself. But one of the other things I think about Dr. Vivian, you know if you want to know something about a man, watch how he treats his wife.

He had the utmost respect, he showed so much love for Octavia. And I could hear him every day saying, "I've got to go see the wife." Dr. Vivian normally used "the wife" to affectionately refer to Octavia. When his wife was sick, he was going every day, I don't care where he was, he had to go to see the wife. He took care of his wife. And he loved her, he treasured her. And that just meant so much to me. To look around and see one of our men, a brother, who respect and love their wife and treasure their wife the way he did. It was just incredible, and I just admired it so much. He's the epitome of a gentleman. And of course we know he's the quiet warrior, the most humble person that you could possibly meet. If all young men could be a C. T. Vivian, just think of where this world would be today.

HANK AARON:

I've been knowing C. T. for a long time. I got to love him, really, not just know him, but love him for what he stood for and what he did and the things that he did. Sometimes you wonder what carried these civil rights guys on. I am so blessed to have known him.

BILLYE AARON:

As I discovered him, his background and all, it just gave me a tremendous appreciation for the man and the work that he was doing. He continued to labor in the vineyard until his death. So I guess you could say, I just felt that it was his destiny. He was destined to become the kind of human being that he was, which was so warm and unassuming. He never stepped out there to try to get in front of the line. He was always working to plan and implement the plan.

JOHN HALLWAS:

Dr. Hallwas, Distinguished Professor Emeritus and Archivist at Western Illinois University, acclaimed author, and friend and admirer of Dr. Vivian, did not attend the funeral. But upon learning that this book was being written, he sent a lovely tribute. Here is an excerpt:

Shortly after the Reverend C. T. Vivian died in the summer of 2020, I learned that he had worked with Steve Fiffer in the last year of his life to write his memoirs. I could not have been more pleased to learn that his own words were captured to tell the story of his magnificent journey throughout his life—a life that I have studied, revered, taught in school, and written about in published articles. Over the years, I have been amazed at his accomplishments, his brilliance, and his writings. Here they are displayed for us to understand more about this man and his mission, to hold on to his words of wisdom throughout our lifetime and to share with generations to come. Here we will learn more about the advocacy, the movement, and the genuine desire based on love to change the world as C. T. Vivian saw it.

Few Americans know much about his life, which is a remarkable story of spiritual growth and social commitment. This engaging memoir provides great insight into both the man and his crucially important cause. It naturally focuses on his efforts for social justice, but his earlier life is a compelling story too. The bright, outgoing boy lived much of the time with his grandmother, Annie Woods Tindell, who taught him how to read before he started school. In 1930 she decided to move to Macomb, Illinois, a town of about eight thousand people, where the schools had been integrated for generations. Western Illinois State Teachers College was located there, so that C. T. eventually would have "the best opportunity to get a college education."

The committed young man realized that his future would be limited without much education, so he also returned to Macomb. Vivian did practice teaching to fulfill his degree requirements at Western, but he ultimately decided to not enter the teaching field. He wanted to study for the ministry, so he and his wife moved to Nashville late in 1954, and he enrolled in the Baptist Theological Seminary, where he received a bachelor's degree three years later. He also served as pastor of the First Community Church from 1956 to 1961.

Over the years he founded or co-founded a variety of educational and civil rights organizations, such as the Black Action Strategies and Information Center and the C. T. Vivian Leadership Institute. And Vivian also lectured and consulted on civil rights and other issues in forty-four states and a dozen foreign countries.

Fortunately, we now have his memoir, which takes us into the heart of his historic effort to advance the Black struggle and to end racial prejudice. *It's in the Action* will surely have an impact for generations to come, depicting C. T.'s life and work—and inspiring others to continue in that crucial cause.

The Eulogy

The Reverend Dr. Gerald Durley, Senior Pastor, Providence Missionary Baptist Church, Atlanta, Georgia:

. . . I believe in all of my heart that we have been summoned to this very sacred place for this consecrated moment to reflect, to remember, a man who never, ever, ever sought the limelight. A man who never wanted to be the center of attention. Today's honoree in fact shied away from the things that others would run to. He was not a "me and my" person, he was always, "Y'all, go ahead and do it."

C. T. never wanted you to tell anything about him and what he did. The Reverend C. T. Vivian always gave the credit to others. I deeply feel that God today has purposely orchestrated this virtual worldwide worship service to highlight and give C. T. Vivian the rightful earned and deserved place as one of the greatest strategists in the civil rights movement.

Today we honor C. T. Vivian. We've honored Martin Luther King, Andrew Young, Joe Lowery, John Lewis, and C. T. was all the way back [with them]. . . . C. T., many times, you might have been left out, many times they might've forgotten you, but you never said, "Look at me. Look who I am." He said, "Give it to 'em" and he gave you that smile. That's who C. T. Vivian was. He never wanted you to say that he stood boldly on his word. He knew who God was, and he knew that God would always give him the praise and the glory.

Dr. Vivian always lifted up and elevated others. He felt that he was a mere catalyst in the human compound of bringing elements together. Dr. C. T. Vivian always looked for the downtrodden people who faced injustice and systemic racism. Today, C. T., you have proven one thing to young people and you need to know, you don't need to be a star football player, you don't need to be a great basketball player or a singer. All you've got to do is be a good person, and good people don't finish last.

C. T. was a good man. Many people knew C. T. Vivian's name, but they didn't know who he really was. . . . And I thought about a word to share today—five simple words that I think epitomize and summarize our honoree, the Reverend Dr. C. T. Vivian. And I could simply say these five words that I call the title, say the benediction, words that come to my mind after reading that passage: *He had a good name.* C. T. Vivian had a good name. . . .

Ninety-five years ago, they labeled a boy Cordy Tindell Vivian and we called him C. T. . . . C. T. had a good name. A good name means that you're stable, a good name says that people can trust you, your word is your honor, your good name says that people can believe in you. . . .

Your good name implies that you're consistent, that your decision can be made in confidence, when you have a good name. A good name speaks volume about your character; a good name says that your character is impeccable; a good name reflects stable, moral, ethical principles, which are the foundations of your life. . . . When we get beyond the labels, we find the good name. It's always not only stable but a good name is eternal. Great riches are fleeting. You get a lot of money here today and gone tomorrow. We rip, we run, we snatch, we lie, we grab, we cheat to get money, more and more money, great riches. We think that we have it when we display all those riches to impress people that don't care a thing about you. As long as the party is on, as long as everybody is happy, they remember your name. But when you get on hard times, when all the money is gone, when you get to the end of the money, that's when you realize they forget your name. Because the money was tied to what you had.

C. T. did not worry about what he had. He never asked for an honorarium. He just said, "When do you want me to come? How do I get there?"

He would walk down a hall and get ready to speak and if three children stopped him, C. T. would stop and start talking to those children and tell the rest of them, "I'll be there in just a minute." Take time! Because he had a good name!

. . . What I've found over the last several days, every time I turn on the television, I'm seeing John Lewis and Joe Lowery and C. T. Vivian. I sit here today, and I heard all of the ministers get up before me and give a sermon about C. T. Vivian, and I listen but I've learned one thing. Everybody sitting here and all of you in television land, each one of you has a C. T. Vivian story. Everybody's got a C. T. Vivian story.

And it's interesting about that story: they're all different, yet they're all the same. When C. T. met you, he was infectious. You thought you were talking to somebody, but he addicted you. Pretty soon you come back and say, "What did he say? What did he mean by that?"

C. T. had to work, he was so smooth, that little smile. Always impeccably dressed, hair just right, and he would be sitting there, C. T.'d be talking to you. C. T. didn't know how to go directly to a story. He went all the way around. Over here, and over there, and you're saying, "Well, I'm going to go pick up my daughter. And he'd say, "That's right, Sis, but let me just say a little thing about that." Or, "Okay, Sis, well, it's good seeing you." But when he got back to the real point, it was always on point.

Everybody had a C. T. Vivian story. . . . Mary Gurley, the great singer from Ebenezer Church who sang for Dr. King, she called me, she said, "I just want to tell you something," and I didn't want to hear another C. T. story because they were trying to sneak in before I could speak their name today. But every now and then a story stands out. She said, "ML and C. T. came to march against the Scripps company years ago. ML had to leave town, but guess what? C. T. stood out there and kept on talking for me." That was her C. T. story.

Young man who had been in prison a long time said, "Let me tell you about C. T. When I got out of jail I didn't know what I was gonna do. One day I came to a major convention and C. T. was walking around out in the lobby, and I looked over and said, 'That's C. T. Vivian, that's the famous C. T. Vivian,' and he's just walking around like normal people."

C. T. was normal! C. T. didn't need an entourage. I don't know what these people need all these bodyguards for. If you need a bodyguard, you don't need to be in the profession you're in. God is your bodyguard. You don't need all these armor-bearers. C. T. didn't need these armor-bearers, because C. T. was covered by God. He feared God.

And this young man said, "And I sat there, and I said, 'Dr. Vivian do you need some water?' And he said, 'Young man, let me get you some water.' He bought me a bottle of water and we talked for over three hours." That was the greatest part, that was his C. T. story.

C. T. would always make you feel like you were the only person in the room. He made you feel, when he talked to you and he looked at you and that little finger would come up, that you were exclusive. And you started feeling good about yourself—*C. T. knows me*. Until he said, "Uh huh, Sis," you found out everybody was "Sis." You thought you were unique.

C. T. had that way. He always said, "You are my pastor." And I said, "How can a pastor pastor a pastor?" But I thought I was good, and my wife said, "C. T. made me feel like a first lady. And I didn't even know what a first lady was." C. T. could make you believe something about yourself. One of the greatest compliments anybody can give to anyone, and C. T. knew it, "You make me feel good about me when I'm with you."

That's the good name that C. T. had. His name will be eternal because of all of the things that he did. Interesting about C. T., you heard about the smile. C. T. would smile, but he never ended with a smile. His smile started most slow, then it got better. Pretty soon he burst out in a laugh. And when C. T. started laughing, you had to laugh too. I remember one time we were talking and he started laughing and I started laughing and I was laughing longer than him, and then I didn't even know what I was laughing at. I didn't even know it was a joke! But it was infectious.

When you're down and lonely and the mountains are high and the valleys are low, you need someone like C. T. to come alongside and say, "You don't know what we've been through, you don't know where we're going."

And he could lift you up. You know when he's lifting you up. Some people lift you up and send you a notice, "Did you get my lift up?" C. T. never did that. C. T. could find the common good in everybody. And if somebody said, whether you were Black, White, tall, gay, straight, whether you walked with a limp, or you were gigantic runner, C. T. found something in you. C. T. didn't look for your earthly label, C. T. looked for the good name in you. And when you put two good names together, that's a winning combination.

His name will live through all of us who are here today. . . . C. T.'s name will live through a program in Alabama called Vision. He believed that young people could do things, and all of you have read the bios and you've heard all of the TV announcements about C. T.'s life, but that was the program out of his mind, out of care and concern and of compassion, where he said, "I want to work with the young people and move to the Upward Bound program."

Some could say, "I never heard about C. T.'s Upward Bound program, because he didn't tell you. He's not gonna tell ya, but maybe some people that graduated from the Upward Bound program might tell you. Denise Morgan, great woman, military person. Viola Davis, Oprah Winfrey, Angela Davis, Donna Brazile, these are all people that came through the Upward Bound program that will keep C. T. Vivian's name alive. They all knew his great name, and they all knew what was expected of him.

C. T. Vivian was the most patient impatient man I knew. He would be patient with you as long as you were doing right. As long as you were going along. But he was impatient with injustice. He was impatient with racism. He was impatient when we took other people down. And as Don [Rivers] or somebody said earlier, none of us in this auditorium or listening round the world could say C. T. ever said a negative or nasty thing about anybody. I pray to God that I could say that at my last homegoing, 'cuz there's some folks I had to just blast [laughter]. Unapologetically blast.

C. T. would say, "Well, they've got a lot of growing to do. Let's pray for them. They really didn't mean what they said." I'd say, "C. T., the man's a fool." And C. T. would answer, "Well, he's not a fool all the time."

C. T. always found the good name, and every time he got knocked down, he got up stronger. C. T. was strong enough to join in with Dr. King and bring all of the affiliates together under SCLC. Now we're talking about inclusion, we're talking about these companies around the world, trying to break down the barriers between Black and White, religious differences.

C. T. founded the first program where he would sit people down and talk above racial line, and he would go in to them and talk and make them feel uneasy. I was in the class of '95 with some of the most powerful people in the city. . . . And one man got up, he was a powerful doctor at Emory. He walked in. He thought he knew everything. He thought he was nonracist. He thought he was something.

And C. T. had us all sit down. C. T. turned over and looked at him and he said, "Hey, I want you to get out of here. You look like a racist." He said, "Dr. Vivian, you don't know me." C. T. said, "You're a racist, get out of here. Look at all of your defenders' races."

And pretty soon we're looking around and I'm sitting there saying, "What's C. T. doing?" He could challenge you, but he only challenged you to make you better in what you were doing. C. T. went on to train pastors and college deans. He was a dean down there at Shaw.

. . . C. T. had a good name. But he married a woman with a *great* name. He married a woman with a great name, and when Octavia walked in the room, he knew, and he'd say, "I didn't know Octavia's name for the first ten years, I just called her 'the wife.'" He said, "Where's the wife?" And I said, "Who's the wife?" But he knew what it was like. He was a role model for my wife and me. We're into fifty-two years of marriage now in a world that is coming apart.

But because of a team and all of the women who were the foundation for those who were out there on the front line—the Kings and the Abernathys, and the Williamses and all of the others—it was the women who were standing there strong, taking care of the children, and talking about what it meant. They had good names because they knew God, and they knew that what they were doing was just as important as those out on the front.

And sometime the children had to sacrifice, the wives had to sacrifice, but because they did, they brought us to this point now in America. So we cannot negate that. She had a good name. She was determined and resolute, but the real key is not just in Proverbs 21:1. Proverbs 22:4. It said that when you humble yourself and when you fear God, he will give you riches, honor, and a long life.

We've come today to celebrate a man who is rich. Oh, Lord, his bank account might not be written that he's got so much in his bank account in his name. But his name was written on the last Book of Life. With all of the funds that he ever needs. All he's got to do is call on God, and when he calls on God, the riches begin to flow.

He's been honored by kings and ambassadors all over the world. But now, today, only a few days from his ninety-sixth birthday, God has given him a long life. He is rich. He has been honored. And now he's received a life. And I say today on behalf of C. T. Vivian, if you want to honor that long life, do what C. T. did when he stood on the courthouse steps there in Dallas County, Selma. We have a moral and an ethical obligation today all over this land if this body has gone to where it's going, then we can keep it alive.

We can keep the good name alive by going out and voting. That's what C. T. would want. He would want us to get up and get out and register and vote and change the nation. Don't shy from that. C. T. was one that said, "I want you to vote. I want you to love your neighbors. I want you to understand that even though I've gone now, I'm happy. 'Scuse me, Octavia, move the chair over, hey, Sis, hey, Corey, hey, Doc."

C. T.—his name is eternal because God gave him a good name and we keep that good name alive by voting. They say in the mortuary business that we all have five senses—we have the sense of touch, we have the sense of sight, we have the senses of smell and taste—but they say when this earthly tabernacle has gone, there is one sense left and that's the sense of hearing. And I believe that even though this body has not been placed to rest, I think right now in the name of Jesus Christ on this great day, we ought to stand and give C. T. Vivian what his due is and he can hear it.

C. T., this is for you. This is your time. Look at the people applauding in this sanctuary. Look at the people up in Washington, D.C., applauding. Look at the people down there in Mississippi and Alabama!

C. T. Vivian, he had a good name. If he was a blessing to you, shout his name! C. T., God bless you.

Appendix 2

He Was Unafraid

Dr. C.T. Vivian's Vita

HIS IMAGE HAS BEEN PLACED IN:

The Civil Rights Institute. Birmingham, Alabama
The National Civil Rights Museum, Memphis, Tennessee
The National Voting Rights Museum, Selma, Alabama
Portrait Hall of Fame, Martin Luther King Jr. International Chapel, Morehouse
    College, Atlanta, Georgia

BOOKS THAT HAVE HIGHLIGHTED HIM:

The Children by David Halberstam
Pillars of Fire by Taylor Branch
Bearing the Cross by David J. Garrow
Parting the Waters by Taylor Branch
Race by Studs Terkel
Odyssey: Journey Through Black America by Earl and Miriam Selby
To Redeem the Soul of America by Adam Fairclough
My Life With Martin Luther King by Coretta Scott King
And the Walls Came Tumbling Down by Ralph David Abernathy
Walking With the Wind by Congressman John Lewis

HE WAS FEATURED IN THE FOLLOWING FILMS AND BROADCASTS:

The Healing Ministry of the Rev. C. T. Vivian on PBS was a full-length feature
    on his life.
The People Century on PBS, a series on the critical issues of the twentieth century,
    depicted him as an analyst and activist.
Eyes on the Prize on PBS was a documentary on the civil rights movement,
    featuring him in several key segments.
King: A Filmed Record . . . From Montgomery to Memphis was a 1970 Oscar-
    nominated documentary that included Dr. Vivian in what is said to be the
    best filmed illustration of nonviolent direct action.
The Oprah Winfrey Show in two episodes in the 1990s featured Vivian in what

147

amounted to a seminar on civil rights and racism; he was the first Oprah guest to be held over for a second day's broadcast due to public demand. He appeared on the show four times.

POSITIONS HE HELD:

Founding member of the board, Capitol City Bank and Trust Company, Atlanta, Georgia.

Board member, Apex Museum, the African American museum of Atlanta, Georgia.

Founding member and board chair, Center for Democratic Renewal (formerly the National Anti-Klan Network), Atlanta, Georgia.

National director of affiliates, Southern Christian Leadership Conference; he served on Dr. King's executive staff throughout the movement years.

Founder, dean of alternative education, and national director, Seminary Without Walls, Shaw University Divinity School, Raleigh, North Carolina, a system of independent, off-campus study offering the bachelor's of theology and the master's of divinity degrees.

Founder and director of Vision, an Alabama educational program that was the prototype for Upward Bound; the sixteen Vision centers trained and placed more than seven hundred teenagers in colleges across the nation.

Director of the Ford Foundation fellowship program, Urban Training Center for Christian Mission, Chicago, Illinois. UTC trained clergy; community leaders and urban activists in methods, techniques, and strategy development.

Founding member, coordinator, and executive director of the Coalition for United Community Action, Chicago, Illinois.

Founding member and president of A Black Center for Strategy and Community Development, Chicago, Illinois. The first African American Center doing strategic and tactical planning for the African American urban community, under African American community control, using African American experts.

Founding member and vice president, Nashville Christian Leadership Conference. Dr. Vivian led the first march of the movement: four thousand persons marching from the Nashville city limits to City Hall was the final action opening public accommodations and citizen participation to all African Americans in the city; NCLC also organized the first Freedom Rides to enter Jackson, Mississippi.

Founder and chairman, Black Action Strategies and Information Center (BASIC). He ran the consultancy for twenty-four years; his son, Al, now president of BASIC, has run the firm for the past twenty years.

INTERNATIONAL LECTURES AND CONSULTANT TOURS

He was a speaker in forty-four of the fifty states, in most U.S. cities, and on four continents and numerous countries.

Africa: He had a month-long odyssey into East and West Africa, especially Kenya and Liberia. He later took agricultural experts to Kenya and made trips in Ghana and Tanzania.

Israel: He had several trips to the Holy Land, including Tel Aviv and Jerusalem; his first trip was as a consultant to KLM Royal Dutch Airlines.

Holland: He made a one-week tour, sponsored by the Christian Youth Council of the Netherlands, to speak to 25,000 youth and appear on national television. His second trip across Holland was on behalf of Amnesty International in advocacy of ending the death penalty.

Manila: He consulted with the National Council of Churches in the Philippines on behalf of the National Council of Churches USA

Brussels: He met with officials of the European Community on issues of human rights and the death penalty.

Japan: He made a nationwide six-week tour after being selected by the Japanese Peace Council to deliver a series of speeches on peace and freedom.

Italy: He had a week-long speaking tour in Rome and the University of Bologna, the oldest university in Europe.

Australia: He had a national speaking tour on issues of justice, race, and peace.

Russia: He made a week-long trip across much of the country.

Lebanon: He had a Peace trip visiting the president, secretary of state, PLO leader Yasser Arafat, and factional leaders.

Cuba: Several speaking trips on nonviolence.

Thailand: Speaker at the World Conference of Religious Leaders in Bangkok.

Other countries: Antigua, Colombia.

ACADEMIC TRAINING

Western Illinois University, B.A.; honorary doctorate
American Baptist Theological Seminary, B.D.
Union of Experimenting Colleges and Universities, Doctoral Program
New School for Social Research, honorary doctorate
Shaw University, honorary doctorate
Morris Brown College, honorary doctorate

BOOKS HE AUTHORED:

Black Power and the American Myth (Minneapolis: Fortress Press), 1970. A bestselling nonfiction social analysis became an Ebony Book Club selection explaining the human and social dynamics of the movement and the effects of strategy, history, and group pressures on Black/White interaction. It was reissued in 2021.

It's in the Action: Memories of a Nonviolent Warrior (Montgomery: NewSouth Books), 2021, is this posthumous autobiography, with Steve Fiffer.

FAMILY

Married Jane Amanda Lee Teague in 1945; they had one child and divorced in 1952. Married Octavia Geans February 23, 1953; they were a devoted couple for fifty-eight years until Octavia's death May 5, 2011.

The Vivians had six children, fourteen grandchildren, twenty-four great-grand-children, twenty-eight great-great-grandchildren, and two great-great-great-grandchildren, as of this writing.

CHILDREN:

Jo Anna (JoJo) Vivian Walker, born November 2, 1945 (with first wife Jane), had five children.

Denise Vivian Morse, born August 9, 1954, had two children.

Cordy Tindell Vivian Jr., born July 19, 1955, died January 30, 2010.

Kira Euzetta Vivian, born October 25, 1956.

Mark Evans Vivian, born August 5, 1958, had four children.

Anita Charisse Vivian, born August 1, 1959, had two children.

Albert Louis (Al) Vivian, born December 20, 1961, had two children.

PRESIDENTIAL MEDAL OF FREEDOM

The nation's highest civilian honor was presented by President Barack Obama, November 20, 2013. The citation reads:

The Reverend C. T. Vivian was a stalwart activist on the march toward racial equality. Whether at a lunch counter, on a Freedom Ride, or behind the bars of a prison cell, he was unafraid to take bold action in the face of fierce resistance.

We salute pioneers who pushed our nation towards greater justice and equality. A Baptist minister, C. T. Vivian, was one of Dr. Martin Luther King Jr.'s closest advisors. "Martin taught us," he says, "that it's in the action that we find out who we really are."

And time and again, Reverend Vivian was among the first to be in the action: In 1947, joining a sit-in to integrate an Illinois restaurant; one of the first Freedom Riders; in Selma, on the courthouse steps to register blacks to vote, for which he was beaten, bloodied, and jailed. Rosa Parks said of him, "Even after things had supposedly been taken care of and we had our rights, he was still out there, inspiring the next generation, including me," helping kids go to college with a program that would become Upward Bound. And at eighty-nine years old, Reverend Vivian is still out there, still in the action, pushing us closer to our founding ideals.

Appendix 3

You Have to Really Love People

The following is an edited transcript of a conversation with the Reverend James Hobart for the Living Legacy Project in March 2015. The occasion was the fiftieth anniversary of the Bloody Sunday March.

JIM HOBART (JH): So, Dr. Vivian, as a child you were growing up in Missouri and in Illinois. Who were the earliest influences in your life regarding your sense of your own self-worth and dignity and rights? And who was it that gave you these messages?

C. T. VIVIAN (CTV): Number One was my grandmother. Now if you're in an African American community, the only person that can—let's put it the other way—your grandmother is as important to you in a Black home as, well, almost as God, right? (laughter) That's where you got most everything you were going to get.

JH: Grandma was sort of God's representative on earth.

CTV: That's true and you may have ten grandmothers, and all of them in their household are the same thing.

JH: Did you have brothers and sisters?

CTV: No, I didn't. No brothers, no sisters, I was making it by myself.

JH: So in those early years you mentioned that your family, school, church, all were what helped to give you your sense of your own worth and dignity.

CTV: Precisely. The church was number one without a doubt. Grandma was really number one, but she's part of the church, and the two go together.

JH: Let me turn that around. If those were the influences positively growing up, what were the earliest experiences with people who were denying you your dignity, your rights, and your self-worth.

CTV: You see, I only became nonviolent later in life. (laughter) Seriously, I have some doubt about how early to start your children as to truly be nonviolent and understanding it. I have a son who has told me that you didn't help me in those first years. He said he took the punishment rather than play with the idea of nonviolence in our neighborhood.

I have to ask myself that—I know exactly the first time someone tried to beat me up. I beat them up. The point being—should I? I'm nonviolent. I am now. The point is, I could whip everyone in my school except a guy in the sixth grade. Nobody beat me up. Now that was interesting, but I didn't want to beat anybody else up. So what I had was nobody was going to fight anybody a grade under them. Now I did not know—that was my first real understanding of my wanting to be what we now call nonviolent. There wasn't a word for it.

JH: You didn't have a concept.

CTV: That's right. Remember Gandhi was somebody we didn't even know about in America. It was really much later in the game.

JH: Let me shift this a little bit. You grew up in Macomb, you went to Western Illinois, but then you left that area and moved to Peoria and you were there at the community center . . . then you decided you were going to be a preacher.

CTV: In fact, I was waiting for the calling for years. In fact, through college, I had already been chosen to go to Colgate. So it wasn't a matter of not wanting to or couldn't—the point being that I believed that you had to be called, and, as a result of that, I was not going to seminary until then.

They gave me a scholarship to Colgate, but then time had passed. I had married and so forth—and now watch that one too. That same son I was telling you about, he wanted to be a minister, but he wanted to be called because I was. In fact his undergraduate work was finished and he went to a seminary up in the hills of North Carolina, and it was Presbyterian, and he said—as we used to say as Black people—"If you're not Baptist, maybe Methodist, somebody's been messing with your religion."

I love the way you shook your head, Sister, you know what we're talking about! The point being that was a kind of basic understanding in that you had to really know what religion is all about or you have no business deciding you are going to be a person for God, and you haven't done anything but decide that it's a nice place to be.

JH: It's gotta be deep, it can't just be in your head, it's gotta be in your heart.

CTV: Precisely. It's got to mean something. In fact, on those types of issues, one thing stands out: what have you done, not what have you thought.

JH: Exactly. Amen (clapping). So you got the call, you found your way to Nashville. And you told me earlier that early on James Farmer was a very important person to you and your development.

CTV: When I was in Peoria—there's years in between. One of the main differences between Black and White churches and ministries is that it's a slow thing for us. Most of us are getting married before we come into ministry. We don't go straight from—you just don't go like you're going from grade school to high school. I met a lot of White guys later on that that is also true of.

When you gave it real meaning, it had to come out of something deeper. When I got the call to the ministry, I had to tell my wife, but the point is I didn't want to because I would be going away to school without an income. She had the only job.

JH: I don't know all the details, but I do know you ended up in Nashville going to school.

CTV: That's right.

JH: And that's where you began to have a connection with James Farmer, was in Nashville?

CTV: James Forman. Farmer was a long time before, because I hadn't left Peoria. See Jim Farmer was ahead of most. There was a movie of Jim. His father knew Greek so well, he sat under a tree on campus and laughed at the Greek jokes. That was Jim. He was trained that way. Jim went to seminary and would not take his diploma.

JH: He wouldn't accept the diploma?

CTV: Because he said it wasn't worth it. What it did not do was just as important as what it did do. Really, what I'm saying to you is this: to most of us, the stuff that others took for granted and liked having and thought that was great stuff wasn't even serious to take.

Jim Farmer graduated and immediately went to the unions because he didn't want to teach something he didn't like or do something that gave no meaning to his life or the life of other people. And that was all of us who were movement people, right. Remember, that was twelve years before Martin. My first actions were twelve years before Martin.

JH: Who emerged in 1955.

CTV: Jim Farmer and the labor unions were talking about real-life issues. How do you deal with how people are going to live? What food can they eat? FDR was there making certain they were fed because other people didn't. You had the CCC—we would not have been able to be ready for any kind of activity as a nation if it had not been for those programs that really gave a chance for those young people to have something.

JH: CCC—Civilian Conservation Corps.

CTV: That's exactly right. When you really see it, you have to think about, what does it mean to be a minister. Is it to have a degree? "Ahh, Momma and Daddy, I have a degree now and can take care of myself."

First time I met Jim, we had a long conversation. He said that he was in a trailer where his office was as a union person, and he says the light was on that night, but he always had the light on, and he says a bullet came through his window but high. Jim said he knew that the guy who shot through the window intended to miss him—because nobody could miss with the light behind him like that. But remember, business people didn't mind killing labor leaders. I can just tell your ages by how you answer questions like that. Because you had to live it. Because you were already in a nation that did not want you if you were poor.

I think that we all need to get ready for what I think is going to be coming, that we're going to see billionaires come together and run it all. And when they run it all, you can bet at the bottom of it is gonna be a lot of people that don't make it and won't make it. And that's where ministry comes in and has meaning; that's where churches that care about people come in.

JH: Just to remind people, CORE [and FOR] organized the earlier Freedom Rides that came down from Washington in [1947]. So Farmer had an impact on your life. So there you are in Nashville, and as I recall

Highlander Folk School is not that far away, I had the good fortune when I was seventeen years old to spend some weeks there in the summertime. One of those transformative events in my life to be in that environment. At that time, the major focus was on labor organizing and education but that was 1952 and very soon began to shift. Can you tell us a little bit about your experience with Highlander and their staff?

CTV: In my case, it was a little later. You've heard the story that Martin was accused of being a communist, and they said that because he was at that ["communist training center"] up there. Why that stands out to me was because I was with Martin at that time there, and he just went there to give a speech. And we left right after he gave the speech—I mean, immediately after. But [the John Birch Society later] had [billboards] up and down the highway accusing him of being a communist, so you knew who owned those coal mines around there. That gives you an idea of the low level of life and how they would put you in jail for nothing and how you also had a hard time getting a job if you talked about helping poor people. I just want you to hear this because if you're younger, you really don't know what's coming.

JH: At Highlander, the music director was Zilphia Horton, the wife of the director of the Highlander Folk School, Myles Horton. She had gone off to South Carolina to organize some tobacco workers and she picked up an old spiritual hymn, and she recast it as "We Will Overcome."

CTV: "We Shall Overcome."

JH: Actually Pete Seeger changed the word "will" to "shall."

CTV: Before Pete Seeger, it was really a gospel hymn and the words of it are far more profound than any before. "If in my heart I do not yield, I shall see God someday." That's the original when it was a gospel song. We made it up on the fields.

JH: Zilphia recast it into "We will overcome." Pete Seeger looked at it and said "shall" is a better word. Then there was a guy named Guy Carawan who got involved with SNCC when he was the music director.

CTV: Let me tell you about that. Guy first came to Nashville—there wasn't any SNCC. SCLC was just getting under way for young people in Nashville. Guy comes in town and—for several years, he taught at a school in California. And he came to South Carolina because he was hunting for the songs and looking for how they were really sung in those days in the backwoods of South Carolina by the people who started it. So Guy learned them the right way—how do you like this (clapping)—"If in my heart, I do not yield, I shall see God someday."

So I got another one for you. Guy made up songs and found songs that were tremendous: "Ain't I Got a Right to the Tree of Life." This is the kind of stuff that the movement produced. And Guy produced it. And no sooner had it become famous, Hollywood gets in on the act, and no one knows that Guy Carawan existed.

We could have had ten movement songs that the nation would have been able to have. But Guy would take his banjo or instrument—I'm from the city, you see—and he'd start tapping his foot, and he'd come up with all these wonderful songs. Every people's movement does more for a nation than a half a dozen different times that you have a new Congress.

JH: Those movements all ride on the peoples' music. Some of us are familiar with a little book called the *Red Book* that the Wobblies [Industrial Workers of the World, a union] put together in the first part of the century. Every movement you look at, whether it be around labor, civil rights, or whatever, and continuing to today, rides on that music as being central to what motivates and energizes.

CTV: Precisely. And just to get my piece in (laughter). Most of that music goes back to spirituals. It goes back to workers again. People who had to be thinking about their humanity and not how much money they were going to make.

JH: I'd like to shift gears right now. Can you tell us about the influences outside of the broad Christian tradition that had an impact on you. I already have a sense of where you might go with that. For example, Gandhi.

CTV: The point being is that it's so important because [America] got to know little or nothing about Gandhi. But do you know who did? People who were suffering. That's why Martin King knew nonviolent direct action. People that were seeking a way to get rid of oppression.

See, Black people were the first to be talking about Gandhi in America. Why? Because we were trying to find a strategy to do what they did to

5

the British because this country was the oppressor, and we had to find a way to convert them. Play with the language. And very, very important is how do you convert people who control the country you're in, control the wealth, control everything else in it, and they're on top and they're in a Wall Street situation, and you think you're going somewhere but you may never get there.

JH: Here's a question playing to the crowd. Someplace along the line, you discovered there were people out there whose religion was Unitarian and Unitarian Universalists. So what could you tell us about what you thought about those people (laughter).

CTV: You're one of the groups I was concerned about! But you were different, and we didn't find the racism with you that we found with most other churches. Can you be a Christian and a racist at the same time? A real Christian?

JH: NO, you can't.

CTV: Because there are only three important words: justice, truth, and love.

JH: Amen

CTV: And if your understanding of religion is so low that you think you can fool God, you have to find a whole other way to live. But the point is they are escaping it. How can you be a racist, hating people, when the central word for all religions, definitely Christianity, is love? How can you then talk about being a Christian?

Because it was about moral and spiritual things. It's not an accident that Martin King had a PhD in philosophical theology, and it's not an accident that he was in the street working with folk and deciding that people had to be free of the problems that were destroying them. It's not an accident; it's knowledgeable. And when we really understand our religion—the basic one in which practically all of us came up on—love is the whole thing.

JH: No religion has the corner on that.

CTV: But that's the point. It's what you do for other people and to other people. That's what it's about. Do you love somebody? That's the major piece. There's been no great religion since Jesus Christ, because he's got it all wrapped up in a thing. I know what you're saying, but if you don't love somebody you have to ask yourself are you religious at all, and it doesn't matter what name is on it.

JH: How did you love Jim Clark down in Selma? Tell us about that!

CTV: I will! I didn't hit Jim Clark. Jim Clark hit me, knocked me down. I got up. You know why? Because God allowed me to. See, I don't play with that stuff. It's serious. Everything I've done in the movement has been because God was with me.

JH: Around that concept of universality of love—one of my educators was my daughter at three years old. She said, "I love you, Daddy, but I don't like you." We can apply that to Jim Clark too.

CTV: You know Jim Clark eventually went to jail. Because he was really breaking the law. Point is he was being paid by people who ran liquor up to Chicago—the same people that said he was a wonderful person were the same people to let him down because they knew he was wrong all the time. I talked to some nuns who were in Selma who came back to do studies on Selma. This woman said it took them twenty years in this town before they came to an understanding that what they were doing was wrong. That's how deep the hate, how deep it all is. Somebody needs to save this society. And we don't have to talk about it like God this, God that. The point is that we have to talk about it like we believe in it.

JH: Talking about nuns reminds me of women.

CTV: Yeah, so far!

JH: Can you reflect for us on the women of the movement, some who weren't as well known as the men, but were also very important. Who can you tell us about?

CTV: A quick way to do it was our wives. My wife cared at the same level that I did, but we had six children and she was more concerned about that than anything else. But she taught them while she was rearing them. When I came home, my wife could've made my children hate me. I was gone all the time, it would've been easy. My wife was very clear when she talked to the kids—the KKK had a group going past our front door and I wasn't home.

JH: Where were you living then?

CTV: Right outside Atlanta, Decatur, Where the big rock is—Stone Mountain. They would go up to Stone Mountain to burn a cross. Oh, great Christians! As a result, they could have come at my wife at any time. My wife wrote a book on Coretta King because she admired Coretta because she knew what Coretta had to put up with.

Here you are and here your husband is gone all the time. You don't know what's going to happen. We get all the honor, but my wife is suffering. Coretta—we see her smiling and laughing but you didn't see it all the time because cameras only take it when they need it. They are the ones that suffer because it's all the time. And they happen to love you. And those are the only people who you know love you, by the way. And if anyone is going to put their life on the line so they can be admired, forget it, because they've forgotten about you two weeks later.

JH: I couldn't agree with you more. In addition to that, in the movement itself there were activist women.

CTV: There were, and they were basically younger and didn't have children.

JH: In Nashville, you must have known Ella Baker and Diane Nash.

CTV: Diane Nash was a student. And you know what I love is that there were more guys involved than women and they voted Diane as leader of the student movement there. When you really love people and you're working for something beyond your own ego, you don't care who's the leader. It's just: are they worth being a leader?

JH: Do you have advice to younger folks and activists about where they ought to be invested in their lives?

CTV: Since you said it and I've been thinking about it, I think so! That's it, until we are ready to love people, we're playing games with ourselves. Gandhi came into London because he beat the British and they knew it and they just wanted to get off looking good. He comes in and they're getting ready to say we've been wrong all the time, and so Gandhi is getting off the plane—and remember back in the days you walk down the steps and onto the dirt—he is walking down the steps. He was in jail for seventeen years. And never gave up the struggle. He won over the whole British Empire who liked to brag that the sun never sets on British soil. We killed everybody who tries not to obey us. Somebody says, "Mr. Gandhi, what do you think of Western civilization." Gandhi looked around, "Who just hollered at me? Oh, it's Jim, how are you? How are your father and mother?" He then said, "What do I think? It would be a good idea!"

JH: Let me ask you a question about a lot of current active movements that have a lot of young people involved—the Occupy movement.

CTV: Problems with it. It didn't do the basic things that a movement has to do. You have to have a strategy—it doesn't matter what it is, will it work? Number two, you have to train your people, and they didn't. You have to understand that you've got to be with it for the length of time, and you have to train your leadership. If you don't, you run into a no-win situation. This is why we have to talk about the mass movements before us. This is why we train people in nonviolent direct action. What Gandhi learned is stuff we have to learn now. We think that since we make money, we are the best people in the world. There's certain principles you've got to know to move people. You have to be able to train people. Occupy went out of business because people stopped coming because they didn't know where you were going, don't see what your aims are. Is it really gonna help anybody? And if it isn't gonna help anybody, then nobody will give their time to it.

JH: The final question I have for you—it's true today that fewer people today are claiming connection to a religious community or even to a particular faith tradition. It might be summarized by that attitude, "I'm spiritual, but not religious." In a situation like this, what might be our new covenant together among the coalition of activists, and is it deep/broad enough to be sustained? Would you reflect on that more?

CTV: If you notice how they keep getting smaller, it comes down to one word—I think I mentioned it a couple of times. This is why Jesus is so important. Love. And then he went further than that. It's loving one another as I have loved you.

It's no golden rule—because it's not really that golden. You have to really love people. Not just a person or two or members of your church.

We can change the world if we love folk. Instead of building a new church, people need to know that somebody loves them. And when people know that, that makes the difference. And that's the people they want to be with.

Audience Questioner (AQ): Dr. Vivian, I would like to ask you about the tremendous training that is now possible at the college level with almost no expense/tuition through University of the People. I'm wondering what you see in this program that allows people to get an accredited bachelor's or associate's degree. Shouldn't our churches/libraries help people get into this training to help them learn ethics and reasoning?

CTV: We had a number of ministers who were not trained so I created a program called Seminary Without Walls, and you could get in with practically nothing. Lilly Foundation gave me the money at that time I needed to develop the idea. It's too precious. Education is too precious to have a great country and uneducated people. People can't live in today's society without knowledge. This is what's wrong with the ghettos. If people can't have an education, don't blame them when they steal! But if you love people, you'll get them an education.

AQ: I'm Amy from New Jersey and teach second grade. Do you think a movement can be successful without music? Without a song that unites?

CTV: Not if you have to organize people on nothing. You've got to have something that makes them more human. And music humanizes everybody. So, No. What we discovered, the better the music, the more people that came. And more people are willing to do. You have cheap music, it doesn't work.

AQ: It seems like many movements today—Occupy—don't have music. The research they're doing on the brain and how music impacts us, I wonder if that's why movements today are not moving.

CTV: When Guy Carawan came along, we didn't have any music. He was White; we were Black. But he was getting Black sources. Everybody fell in love. It makes a difference because you've got to make people know that you believe they are more human than it seems. You are human enough to understand them—you've got to let them know. Don't think you can just stand in front of people and read a book.

AQ: Linda White from Peoria. I recently read that Dr. King said you were the best preacher he'd ever heard. What is it about your style that's so compelling?

CTV: At that time, I preached like preachers really preach but with sense. (laughs)

JH: Something all of us preachers can aspire to.

CTV: That's why that happened, but I'm always chagrined when people come up with that line. I've heard too many great preachers.

AQ: I'm working with the Black Lives Matter movement. How do we prepare ourselves for the road being long? We talk about burn-out and how do we share leadership so we're not all exhausted at once. What advice can you give me and my comrades to keep energized?

CTV: Get all the knowledge you can. Find out about all the leaders that have been around. Martin got his basic stuff from Gandhi, who was not Black. Get the best leadership stuff you can get. Let people know that you really care for them. I keep coming back to that because it's the number one thing. And tell them why. Let them know that's the way to live. That's what the church should be doing.

Sources

All direct quotations are attributed in the text, but their sources are noted here as well, along with other helpful resources.

INTERVIEWS WITH DR. VIVIAN

These can be found on the Internet in video and/or transcript form.

National Visionary Leadership Project, which shares stories of extraordinary African American elders, offers ten short interviews with Dr. Vivian on different milestones in his life.

The History Makers, the nation's largest African American video oral history collection, interviewed Dr. Vivian about his life for several hours in 2004 and 2016.

The Library of Congress commissioned Pulitzer Prize-winning historian Taylor Branch to conduct a lengthy interview with Dr. Vivian in 2011. It is available in video and as a PDF.

The Living Legacy Project, which captures stories of the civil rights movement and the Unitarian Universalist role in it, provides an interview between board member the Reverend James Hobart and Dr. Vivian on the occasion of the fiftieth anniversary of Bloody Sunday in March 2015. A recording can be accessed on the Marching in the Arc of Justice web page by clicking on the resources tab.

Eyes on the Prize, the award-winning PBS documentary on the civil rights movement, was a major source for the book's discussion of the Nashville Student Movement and the Freedom Rides, as well as other events in Dr. Vivian's life. The transcript of his interview with the filmmakers, digitalized at Washington University in St. Louis, can be found at www.digital.wustl.edu in the Eyes on the Prize Interviews Collection, as can an interview with Diane Nash.

OTHER BOOKS

Taylor Branch's award-winning trilogy on "America During the King Years" is must reading. The three books are *Parting the Waters*, *At Canaan's Edge*, and *Pillar of Fire*.

The Black Man: His Antecedents, His Genius, and His Achievements by William Wells Brown.

Furious Cool: Richard Pryor and the World That Made Him by co-authors David and Joe Henry.

Becoming Richard Pryor by Scott Saul.

Freedom Riders: 1961 and the Struggle for Racial Justice by Raymond Arsenault.

Racial Change and Community Crisis: St. Augustine, Florida, 1877–1980 by David R. Colburn (the book was a primary source for material offered by the Martin Luther King, Jr. Research and Education Institute at Stanford University).

The Children by David Halberstam.

The Chicago Freedom Movement: Martin Luther King Jr. and Civil Rights Activism in the North, edited by Mary Lou Finley, Bernard Lafayette, James R. Ralph Jr., and Pam Smith.

Jimmie Lee & James: Two Lives, Two Deaths, and the Movement that Changed America by Steve Fiffer and Adar Cohen.

Black Power at Work: Community Control, Affirmative Action, and the Construction Industry, edited by David A. Goldberg.

NEWSPAPERS, MAGAZINES, AND OTHER WRITTEN MATERIAL

The archives of the *New York Times* and the *Nashville Tennessean* were particularly helpful in chronicling events in St. Augustine (1964) and Nashville (1960).

Ernie Suggs's remarkable piece of reporting, "The Freedom Fighter: How Atlanta's C. T. Vivian Changed History," appeared in the *Atlanta Journal-Constitution* on July 26, 2017. It can be accessed at www.ajc.com.

Rick Harmon of the *Montgomery Advertiser* compiled "Timeline: the Selma to Montgomery Marches," that was published in *USA Today* on March 5, 2015, on the fiftieth anniversary of Bloody Sunday.

Interview with James Farmer by Robert Penn Warren, from Warren's 1965 book, *Who Speaks For the Negro?* A full collection of the interviews is available at www.whospeaks.library.vanderbilt.edu.

The "Vision Alabama Tutorial Project" pamphlet can be found on the website of the Lowcountry Digital Library.

The "National Register of Historic Places: American Baptist Theological Seminary Historic District" offers a good history of the movement's ABTS roots.

Will Globalization Play in Peoria? Class, Race, and Nation in the Global Economy, 1948–2000 is the dissertation of Jason Kozlowski, PhD, and is available from ResearchGate.net.

"The Rise and Fall of the 1969 Chicago Jobs Campaign: Street Gangs, Coalition Politics, and the Origins of Mass Incarceration," an entry in the *University of Memphis Law Review* (vol. 49), by Toussaint Losier, can be accessed at www.memphis.edu.

"Faith in Black Power: Chicago's Urban Training Center for Christian Mission, 1966–1970" by Erik Gellman is a paper presented at the American Historical Association conference, Chicago, January 5–8, 2012.

Index